THE BEST LITTLE GUIDEBOOK FOR TREKKING THE EVEREST REGION

ALONZO L. LYONS

Nepal Insider Editions

ISBN-13: 978-1502421340

ISBN-10: 1502421348

Advisory

As with any activity in a foreign country, both seen and unseen risks exist. Every effort has been made to provide precise material. Although, in a constantly changing world, the author cannot guarantee accuracy of the information in this guidebook. Safety is always the reader's responsibility.

There have been occasional reports of harm to tourists in Nepal. The rare incidents usually happen to lone trekkers. Please do not trek alone.

Nepal experienced an internal conflict from 1996-2006, and a peace accord was signed in 2006. Despite recent global economic upheaval, tourist arrivals continue to grow.

Visitors are encouraged to check with respective embassies to keep up with travel precautions and advisories.

Trekking is an experience of a lifetime. Good-speed and keep on trekking!

Contents

.

INTRODUCTION

The Khumbu (Everest Region of Nepal) and its highland World Heritage Site, Sagarmatha National Park, are graced with many natural attractions and highlights that will compete for your attention every step of the way! This mountain lover's Nirvana is as good as it gets for Himalayan trekking and mountain scenery. The region boasts more well-endowed vistas than you will likely have in your entire life. The land is populated by a fascinating people following a timeless way of life, the Sherpa. Known as *Tigers of the Snow* for their climbing abilities, Sherpa are the local guardians of the Himalaya and trusted climbing partners in the mountains that they consider divine.

There are many treasures to explore in this Sherpa Homeland favored by Mother Nature including the historic setting of Everest Base Camp, dazzling Gokyo Lakes, the ambitious Three Passes Circuit and inviting side-tours. Khumbu is an exhilarating land filled with continuous views of majestic peaks -- a trekker's Shangrila! Whichever routes and destinations you choose, the culture, regal monasteries, radiant mountains, delicious home-style nourishment and swill, welcoming residents and a posse of fellow international travelers combine to make a trek in the Everest Region a lifetime Highlight.

Recommended First Step: Trek into the Sherpa Homeland (Rather than Flying to Lukla)

Trekking in to the Everest Region not only assists in acclimatization, but is a magnificent introduction to the lifestyle and culture of the mid-hills of Nepal. A daylong, scenic drive from Kathmandu reaches Jiri, typical starting point for a hike to the elevated homeland of the Sherpa. This classic route follows the footsteps of mountaineers who long ago passed through the same emerald lowlands en route to the barren, alpine nirvana of the Khumbu.

The trek contours fertile landscape before eventually reaching the desolate highlands harried by freezing storms, yet soaked by sunlight, a land filled with snowy masterpieces beloved by climbers, including the grandest of all Everest, jutting into the heavens.

PRE-ARRIVAL PREPARATIONS

Physical preparedness will add to your enjoyment of this exhilarating experience. Travelling up to and along the ramparts of the Himalaya is a vigorous activity that requires fitness and stamina. A training regimen is strongly advised prior to arriving to Nepal. The hills and valleys on the way up to and within the incomparable Everest Region are steep and the high elevation and thin air makes exertion all the more strenuous. In fact, even when you are descending, in the Everest Region it might seem like an *uphill* grind.

If you are fit and fine, then a journey into the Khumbu highlands will be all the more enjoyable and satisfying. Adding rest and acclimatization days is essential and will improve the overall trekking experience.

Even for people in excellent physical shape, the world's highest trails sometimes take perseverance and grit, and pre-arrival efforts to get in physical shape before the trek will be handsomely rewarded. Practice on your own regional hills with a pack and boots before reaching Himalayan territory that will ultimately be higher and steeper than anything you have seen back home -- anywhere on earth!

Although mountains belong to the nation, mountains really belong to the people who love them. – Mountain and Water Sutra, Dogan, 13th Century Zen Master

The Responsible Traveler

Summary: Even a brief meeting with a traveler can have a deep and lasting effect for local people. Nearly everything a visitor says and does in a rural area will be observed and talked about long after the tourist leaves. Travel responsibly and set yourself apart. Doors will be opened to friendships and extraordinary cultural experiences in this enchanting land. A common theme for trekkers is that 'The Himalaya may change you, please do not change them.'

Most travelers have seen and experienced more of the modern world than a person living in the remote hills of Nepal. What you say and do and how you dress will likely be novel and different and can have a strong influence and lasting impact on the people you meet as well as the people in their circle and beyond to visitors who will follow your footsteps. Nepali culture is very hospitable and agreeable. Act decently and you will easily be accepted. Be a respectable traveler and you will make the experience better for everyone, especially yourself.

There are a few easy guidelines for the responsible traveler in the Himalaya. Dressing as modestly as Nepalis will be a great first step to cultural acceptance. Respond to greetings with a 'Namaste', eat using your right hand and do not share tableware and drinking containers that have touched your lips. Do this and you will be well on your way to meeting basic cultural norms. Please do not show physical affection. Hand-holding by members of the opposite sex and couples kissing in public is inconceivable to most Nepalis.

If you play a musical instrument, consider bringing it along to ease communication barriers. Nepalis are generally great lovers of song and dance. Consider other social and entertainment skills that you might share, for example, portrait sketching and simple card tricks.

LEAVE NO TRACE IN THE HIMALAYA by following four fundamental rules

• Dispose of Waste Properly ('Pack It In, Pack It Out')

• Leave What You Find

• Respect Wildlife and Farm Animals

• Be Considerate of Others, Local Customs and Traditions

The Annapurna Conservation Area Project and Kathmandu Environmental Education Project recommend the responsible traveler to follow a **Minimum Impact Code**:

• Encourage lodges and trekking companies in their efforts to conserve environmental resources.

• Campfires and hot showers are a luxury when locals use fuel for cooking only.

• Use washing and toilet facilities provided, or, if none are available, make sure you are at least 30 meters (100 ft) from any water source. Bury excreta at least 15 cm (6 in) and use biodegradable toiletries.

• Limit your use of non-biodegradable items and pack them out.

• Respect religious shrines and artifacts.

• Don't give money, sweets or other materials to begging children.

• Taking photographs is a privilege, not a right. Ask permission and respect people's desire not to be photographed.

• Dress modestly and avoid outward displays of physical affection.

- You are a representative of another culture and your impact lingers long after you return home.

The Kathmandu Environmental Education Project (KEEP) maintains a Porter's Clothing Bank, and other resources including trekker logbooks with the latest trail information and supplies such as water purifiers, anti-leech oil, biodegradable soap, and more.

While trekking, if the desire to donate money or materials along the way is tempting, the following from The Center for Responsible Travel (http://www.responsibletravel.org/home/index.html) provides valuable guidelines for those wishing to make a difference while traveling:

"Travelers' desire to help, interact, and learn from those they meet during their holiday is clearly positive. However, there are sometimes unintended consequences from these good intentions. Misguided contributions can perpetuate cycles of dependency, cause corruption, burden communities with unwanted or inappropriate donations, and require recipients to spend time and resources to handle 'gifts' they didn't request or cannot use...when, how, and what to contribute needs to be decided by the host community, not the tourist or the tourism company."

WHEN TO GO

The busiest months for Sagarmatha National Park, in decreasing order, are October, April, November, March, September, and May.

Summary: Nepal has four main seasons. The most popular for tourism is autumn (October to November), just after the monsoon rains when the hills are replenished and lush. The relatively cleaner air offers vibrant views. Spring (March to May) is next in popularity, a time when Nepal's world famous rhododendrons are in bloom. Most people avoid the rainy months (June to September) and the cold winter months (December to February), but each season has something special and different to offer.

Weather is one of the most important factors to consider when planning a visit to the Himalaya. Each of the four seasons of Nepal is unique from the others with each having something special to offer. A trip during the monsoon will be completely unlike an autumn journey which will be different from spring and winter.

The most popular season is autumn (October to November) when the rains have washed the skies and weather and views are superior, followed by spring and then winter. Most people avoid the rainy months when constant cloud cover hinders views and leeches thrive in the highlands. Similarly, most people are not keen to trek in the winter when the temperature is too cold for comfort at high elevations and snows can block high passes through April and into May.

The main routes are busy in October and November and the reason is understandable: vibrant mountain views and reliable weather. This is the season when climbers push for the summits. If you have already visited Annapurna, Everest, and Langtang, you might want to escape the crowds on the main trails and try more off-beat trekking. October is the time of rice harvesting and *Dasai*, Nepal's most important festival that is followed by the festival of lights, *Tihaar*. This is a great time to immerse yourself in the culture of the mid-hills.

December, January and February, are coldest and haze often sits in valleys and reaches up to the ramparts of the Himalaya, too, diminishing views. During this season, lower elevation trails (3,500 meters and below) are suggested. If you ascend higher, then be prepared for temperatures below freezing, fog in the mornings, and the possibility of snowfall. You will have the trails more or less to yourself, peaceful but physically demanding!

March, April and May are also preferred months for high-altitude treks and climbing. However, the lowlands are less pleasant at this time as temperatures will be too warm for comfort. The dry weather air can be dusty and polluted and views obscured. May is the month immediately prior to the beginning of the monsoon of June, and rainfall will occasionally threaten and cloud cover can be expected.

The above outlined seasons of Nepal are the best for trekking, and generally people avoid the rainy season unless going into the rain shadow areas north of the Himalaya. The monsoon typically begins in June and finishes by October, but frequently continues later. If you are prepared for rain, then it can be a memorable time to be in the mountains. Rain and fog can be expected almost daily, and clouds rarely part, and when they do they offer unforgettable views of the mystical mountains and surroundings.

Generally, more rain falls in the east of Nepal as the monsoon arrives there from the Bay of Bengal and moves westward. Despite the lack of mountain vistas, the monsoon season is undeniably a beautiful time of year when the general haze of pollution is absent. Plants are at their greenest, trails are lined by wildflowers and meadows are swarming butterflies. Waterfalls are roaring at this time, too. Commonly, rain drizzles off and on throughout the days. When it arrives, people find the nearest shelter and wait it out, as downpours usually do not last long—although some last for several days continuous! Keep in mind that you and your gear will likely get wet. Trails can be muddy and slippery. It will be hot and humid. Roads, trails, and bridges may wash out with time-consuming and difficult detours. To make matters more challenging, leeches are active above 1200 m. A sense of adventure and certain items of equipment are essential: a waterproof cover for your pack, sheets of plastic for covering porter loads, an umbrella, a hat with brim, a walking stick or ski pole, and footwear with good traction.

Whenever you choose to visit, each of the seasons of Nepal has something unique and special to offer and makes Nepal a year-round destination.

Clearest Views: October to November
Next Best: March to May
Cold Winter: December to February
Monsoon: June to September

Rise and fall of Temperature in the Khumbu

Under normal atmospheric conditions, the lapse rate, the rate the temperature drops as altitude is gained is generally 3.5°F per 1000 feet (6.4°C/km). This is an estimate dependent on a number of factors. Under dryer conditions the lapse rate is greater than when humid. Additionally, the lay of the land will have intervening factors that affect temperature including the direction the slope faces (i.e., north facing slopes receive less sunshine and therefore are generally cooler), amount of cover by vegetation - trees that provide shade, other objects that provide shade (e.g., a Himalayan peak between your location and the sun), and presence of waterways. The snow line in the Khumbu is around 6000 meters on south facing slopes and 200 meters lower on cooler, north facing slopes. The tree line is about 4,000 m. Mountainous walls and ridges that surround Khumbu valleys protect them to some extent against cold winds from Central Asia and monsoon rains from the Bay of Bengal, and high elevations are generally drier because cold air does not readily retain moisture.

THE EVEREST REGION

Khumbu is the northern section of Solu–Khumbu District. The area includes the World Heritage Site (Natural) of Sagarmatha National Park featuring Mount Everest as well as two other 8000-meter (26,247-foot) peaks, Lhotse (27,890 feet, 8501 m, fourth highest in the world) and Cho Oyu (26,906 feet,8201 m, sixth highest). Sagarmatha National Park borders the Tibetan Frontier, and to the east is Makalu (27,765 feet, 8463 m, fifth highest) in neighboring Makalu-Barun National Park.

The elevated terrain of the Khumbu and its hidden valleys were considered by Guru Rinpoche (aka, *Padmasambhava*, an eighth century mystic referred to by Tibetans as 'the Second Buddha'), to be a preserve of harmony and refuge away from the world's commotion and confusion. More than 90% of Khumbu and its sacred valleys are above 3500 m (11,500 ft). The land is sparsely populated by Sherpa people, an ethnic group with origins on the Tibetan plateau. Known as the *Tigers of the Snow*, Sherpa are famed for their stamina and skill on climbing expeditions on the world's highest peaks. Tenzing Norgay Sherpa from Thame village of the Khumbu teamed up with Edmund Percival Hillary for the first ascent of Everest on May 29[th,] 1953. The feat was announced around the globe and sparked worldwide interest in Nepal and the Himalaya. Nowadays, climbing Nepal's majestic peaks has grown into a thriving industry but not without controversy of who should be allowed on the mountains (money plays its usual strong role). Everest is locally known as *Chomolungma* (a Tibetan name of the Goddess that resides there) and *Sagarmatha* (Nepali name that roughly translates to the top of the planet reaching the ocean of the heavens), and its classic base camp route is the premier destination for most trekkers in a region with much to explore.

The main trekking routes include four remote valleys with three challenging mountain passes connecting these valleys. The three passes will be described within this guide along with the classic trekking routes in the Khumbu highlands. The original gateway route begins at Jiri in *Solu*, the southern section of the Solu-Khumbu Distric, or the next village of Shivalaya beyond Jiri (and possibly the idyllic Bhandar depending on road conditions—however, the ride into Bhandar is not a pleasant one, even under the best of conditions and should be avoided unless you are absolutely pressed for time.) The hike from Jiri or Shivalaya is recommended for both nature and culture, and if nothing else, the legs and lungs will be invigorated for the uplands of the Khumbu. This hike to the Khumbu takes up to ten days with many scenic hills, valleys and ravines traversed along the way.

Nowadays, most visitors to the Everest Region fly into the mountain village of Lukla at a high elevation airfield (2850 m, 9350 ft), shortening the journey to the Khumbu and increasing considerably the likelihood of acute mountain sickness (please see the section on Altitude Sickness for more information). Those who walk in will be much more acclimatized as they climb into rarefied air. Lukla is a day and a half south of Namche Bazaar, the gateway to the Khumbu Region. Other options to enter Solu-Khumbu include,

-walking from the Arun Valley to the east

-flying into Paphlu Airport (a two days walk southwest of Lukla)

-taking a recently built road to Paphlu and beyond towards Ringmo (a rough, tiring vehicle ride from Kathmandu that will test both physical and mental stamina).

Whichever entry route you choose, a journey into enchanting Solu-Khumbu will be the trek of a lifetime. Enjoy the well-endowed natural splendor with surrounding Himalayan titans and magnificent village scenery with welcoming people.

Getting Started

In the route descriptions that follow, **times do not include stops**. That is, only actual hiking time has been provided. Overall times, including stops (for tea and snacks, photography, resting, et cetera), are longer than indicated times.

Additionally, trail conditions and routes can change for a variety of reasons and there may be inaccuracies in the following description. When trails do change, it is usually because of a landslide, erosion and damage and finding more suitable routes as well as the result of rapid road construction taking place throughout Nepal.

During the winter season, there is less daylight than at other times. Everyone has their own rhythm, but regardless of season, most people finish the day's trekking before 5 PM and depart mid- to late morning, after breakfast.

Altitudes listed in the descriptions are taken from several sources, including maps and GPS readings.

KHUMBU HIGHLIGHTS

best time to visit: Post-monsoon from late-September to November when the weather is clearest and most reliable. Pre-monsoon from March to May is another window of opportunity for decent weather.

environment: mid-hills to high elevation river valleys and alpine highlands with a feast of snowy Himalayan peaks at every turn.

maximum elevations: Kala Pattar (5550 m/18,208 ft), Gokyo Ri (5360 m/17,585 ft), Kongma La (5527 m/18,135 ft), Cho La (5420 m/17,783 ft), Renjo La (5375m/17,634 ft), Kongde Ridge (4200 m/13,80 ft)

facilities: hotels, teahouses, gear shops, outlet stores, bakeries, restaurants, pubs, billiard halls (especially lively in Lukla, Phakding and Namche)

duration: up to two weeks and more depending on travel style, side-trips and route choices

difficulty level: moderate to extreme given the high elevation and remoteness of the Khumbu; acclimatization is very important for safety here!

Formalities: Nepal Visa ($30 to $100 USD on arrival), Sagarmatha National Park Permit (3000 NRS), Trekking Information Management System Card ($20 USD equivalent). *Advisory: Advisory: If walking in from Jiri/Shivalaya/Bhandar, then arrange the Sagarmatha National Park permit and TIMS card in Kathmandu. Still, you might have to pay a fee (2000 NPR) for passing through a section of the Gauri-Shankar National Park along the way!*

costs: $20 to 25 USD/day and up, not including guide and porter (prices generally increase with elevation)

typical dishes: *daal-bhat tarakari* (heaping plate of rice with lentil soup and curried vegetables), *shyakpa stew* (a Sherpa favourite -- bowl of handmade noodles with potatoes and other seasonal vegetables), *tsampa* (buckwheat or barley flour mixed with hot water or *solja*, salt-butter tea, with perhaps a side of lentils or vegetables and eaten as a doughy paste), potatoes (in many variations) and westernized dishes.

typical beverages: *chiyaa* (sweet milk tea); *solja* (salt-butter tea, largely an acquired taste); fermented spirits *chhyang* (not distilled) and *roxy* (distilled)

highlights: alpine scenery, highest peak and mountain range on the planet, Sherpa culture, regal Buddhist monasteries, Everest Base Camp, meeting international travellers, ancient villages, scenic vistas from the world's best viewpoints, remote passes, highland pastures, sparkling lakes, rushing rivers and streams, plummeting waterfalls, local food and drink, yaks (and possibly yetis).

ENTERING THE EVEREST REGION

Welcome to a hiking odyssey along the ramparts of the Himalaya in the world famous Everest Region. This area has some of the world's most scenic and exhilarating routes, with continuous mountain views competing for your attention and cultural highlights along the way. You can feast on native, home-style dishes and still experience a timeless way of life, meet a united nations of friendly co-travelers and all while enjoy a lifetime's worth of inspiring mountain vistas. Welcome to trekker's paradise, the Everest Region.

The classic route, following the footsteps of original mountaineers to the region, is to hike all the way from Kathmandu Valley. Such a journey follows in the famous footsteps of Hillary, Norgay and crew (the legendary first team to summit Everest). Nowadays, few people start from Kathmandu. Although it remains a transcendent journey, roads and vehicle traffic along the way make it impractical.

Roadways are under construction throughout Nepal including rural tracks reaching ever closer to the Khumbu. Jiri, Shivalaya, and Bhandar are typical starting points for the trek that can be reached in a scenic, daylong bus ride from the Old Bus Park (also known as Ratna Bus Park) in central Kathmandu.

Hiking in to Solu-Khumbu from these villages will greatly broaden the experience both culturally and in exhilirting natural scenery. The fertile landscape along the way with ancient villages surrounded by emerald and golden paddy fields cannot be experienced in the rugged territory above Lukla (the high elevation airport where most people arrive by plane).

Nowadays, trekkers hiking in usually begin from Shivalaya, a quiet hamlet whose name literally means 'the abode of Shiva'. Starting from Jiri will lessen the drive (to Shivalaya) by a few hours but lengthens the hike by half a day. The ride on to Bhandar from Shivalaya will take several more hours but will save half a day's hike on a steep uphill and downhill section of trail.

Most travelers choose the time-saving option of flying to Lukla (2850 m, 9350 ft), a day south of the Sagarmatha National Park Boundary, entryway to the Khumbu. Flying in places visitors closer to the soaring peaks and lessens the hike from Jiri by about a week but increases concerns of acute mountain sickness. Some travelers even charter helicopter service to Syangboche (3720 m, 12,205 ft), the airfield above Namche Bazaar, but rapid ascent to the thin air of this altitude is precarious, and can be fatal if the body cannot adjust.

Many people choose to fly one segment to Lukla and hike the other to Jiri or Shivalaya. If you choose this option, it is advised to hike in and save the flight for the way out to better acclimatize while entering the highlands. Whether flying into or out of Lukla, then keep in mind that during the high seasons, delays occur, especially when weather deteriorates and aircraft are grounded causing holdups and even cancellations. To avoid the stress and dilemma of being late for connecting travel, leave an extra margin of time in your schedule between a flight from Lukla and international departure from Kathmandu. Air service to/from Phaphlu, a two days walk from Lukla, provides additional options in a pinch (and Phaphlu has road service, too, but be prepared for a long, rugged ride).

For people hiking in from the road, the trail and facilities on the Jiri-to-Lukla trail offer a chance to savor a relatively calmer and uncrowded route compared to Lukla and above. If you trek in, obtain a Sagarmatha National Park permit and TIMS card in Kathmandu, and even then, you might be obligated to purchase a Gauri-Shankar Conservation Area permit in Shivalaya for passing through the southern fringes of that park.

Prices soar as you trek higher (along with elevation). Expect to spend a minimum of $15–$25 USD per day (1100 to 1500 NRS) starting from Lukla, and around two-thirds of that amount up to Lukla. Bring more for contingencies. Additionally, you will find better bargains away from the popular overnight waypoints that are recommended in guidebooks and fill up quickly.

For an infusion of cash while on the journey, banking and money-changing facilities exist in Lukla and Namche, and a few hotels can provide a cash advance on credit cards -- with an exorbitant transaction fee. The few ATMs in the region are not reliable and often out of commission.

An adventurous back-route option to enter/depart the Khumbu region traverses its westernmost village of Thame via Rolwaling and a high pass, the Trashi Labsta (18,947 feet, 5775 m). This thrilling route is hazardous for rock fall and crevasses. Technical equipment is needed and self-sufficiency in food and gear. A seasoned guide is advised. Once over the Trashi Labsta, the route traverses remote sections of Rolwaling, a rare gem with few facilities for trekkers. The journey eventually reaches feeder roads to the Kathmandu–Kodari road to Tibet and the road to Chaurikot which lies along the highway to Jiri.

Please keep in mind that casualties occur in the Khumbu every year from altitude sickness. It is essential to take time while going up and listen to your body's signals. The Himalayan Rescue Association (HRA) offers lectures on acclimatization and altitude sickness in Pheriche (and neighboring Dingboche). Pheriche also has a seasonal HRA clinic and consultations with doctors can be arranged for the equivalent of $50 USD, credit cards accepted. Additionally, a rescue outpost in Machherma provides informative lectures and treatment. It was established by the International Porter Protection Group and is seasonally staffed by international volunteers.

ROUTE DETAILS

JIRI TO THE KHUMBU (7-9 Days)

Walking to the Khumbu is a thrilling experience along trails very different from the crowded pathways above Lukla, Namche, and beyond. The average hiking time to Namche Bazaar is 7–9 days from Jiri, but if you are feeling fit and fine and willing to push it with long days, then it is possible cover the journey in 4 or 5 days. The trails to Lukla traverse west to east with a succession of ups and downs. The ridges crossed are high and the rises and falls of the trails are steep and strenuous. The benefits to hiking in include a great chance to get in shape for the higher terrain and thinner air of the Khumbu.

Advisory: If walking in from Jiri or Shivalaya, obtain a Sagarmatha National Park entry permit and TIMS card in Kathmandu before departure. The check post in Shivalaya for the Gauri-Shankar Conservation Area might still try to assess a fee for passing through the southern fringes of that park! Shivalaya is the recommended starting point for hiking in to the

Khumbu. Options incuding Shivalaya are the following:

A. Most trekkers begin from Shivalaya although Jiri and Bhandar are options. Starting from Jiri will lessen the drive by a few hours but lengthen the walk by half a day.

It is a grueling vehicle ride to Bhandar from Shivalaya and takes several hours but saves a day compared to starting from Jiri and saves about a half day from starting in Shivalaya and avoids a steep hike.

B. Flight or vehicle to/from Phaphlu…Phaphlu is a two day walk to/from Lukla (the drive into or out of Salleri/Paphlu is not advised – too rugged and long).

C. Flight to Lukla, high mountain airfield that is a day hike from the Sagarmatha National Park boundary (be on the lookout for signs of AMS!).

D. Hike in from the Arun Valley to the east.

DAY 1 - **To the Trail Head at Jiri or Shivalaya**
Start: Kathmandu 1336 m
End: Jiri 1905 m or Shivalaya 1790 m
Time: 7+ hrs
Highlights: scenic drive through terraced farmland, lush jungle, glimpses of snowy peaks

---

The typical starting points of Jiri, Shivalaya, and Bhandar are reached in a scenic daylong bus ride from the Kathmandu's Old Bus Park (also known as Ratna Bus Park).

From Kathmandu, take one of the buses heading to Jiri or Shivalaya (or possibly even Bhandar, depending on road conditions, which will save a day or two for people with time constraints, but is a rough, unpleasant ride). Old Bus Park (aka, Ratna Bus Park) is east of Tundikhel parade ground in the central section of Kathmandu.

Do not expect to have time to trek after the bus ride. The journey is about 190 km (120 miles) and takes much of the day and can be exhausting due to uncomfortable seats and road conditions. Buses depart as early as 5:30 am. Or hire a private vehicle for around 20,000 NRS and up (return vehicles back from Jiri to Kathmandu are difficult to arrange unless a taxi has just dropped someone and the driver is looking for a return fare).

The road journey passes a police post on the final descent into Jiri where you will be required to register your trekking and passport details. Jiri (6250 feet, 1905 m) has a busy bazaar area and several choices for accommodation as well as a hospital, technical colleges and below town is an agricultural center developed with Swiss assistance.

Jiri to Shivalaya

The hike to Shivalya and Bhandar can be a bit of a scramble because of the roadway intersecting the trail and other trails overlapping the route. When in doubt, keep to the widest track and ask locals for the way to Shivalaya.

Start from the south end of the bus park in **Jiri**, and follow the road (which continues to a village named Those 'Toe-say'and on to Shivalaya) for ten minutes before branching left at a signed junction, although the signs there might not be too clear. Begin your climb through a rhododendron thicket to tea shops at Bagkhor and then Ratomate to a lodge at Chitre. Ascend to the east to a relay tower at the pass (7875 feet, 2400 m), **2-2½ hours** from Jiri. **If the weather is clear, then from here you have inspiring, initial views of the snowy peaks.**

Pass down through a pine grove to Mali with shops and a lodge. Continue descending with more shops and lodging to a bridge over the Yelung Khola, crossed to the northeast (left) bank. Contour and shortly thereafter, cross a suspension bridge over the Khimti Khola to **Shivalaya** (5873 feet, 1790 m), **2 hours** from the pass.

The name Shivalaya translates to *'Abode of Shiva'* and is auspiciously named for the Hindu deity Shiva (despite the Hindu name, the hamlet also hosts a Christian Church, more and more common in rural Nepal due to proactive missionary activities). A Hindu shrine stands on a finger of land at the east end of the busy market. Shivalaya has several lodges to choose from and a police check post and a Gauri-Shankar Conservation Area check post, too. Shivalaya is at the southern fringes of this newly designated (2011) Gauri Shankar Conservation Area, and the trail of the Numbur Cheese Circuit begins here and follows north up the Khimti Khola. Unless you have a Sagarmatha National Park permit and TIMS card, then the conservation area staff will bid you to purchase a Gauri-Shankar Conservation Area permit for 2000 NRS, even if you have no intention of heading deeper into that conservation area. If you present your Sagarmatha permit and TIMS card, then they should leave you alone to dodge the Gauri-Shankar fee.

DAY 2 – SHIVALAYA TO BHANDAR
Start: Shivalaya 1790 m
End: Bhandar 2194 m
Time: 3¼–4¼ hrs
Highlights: distant glimpses of peaks, rural vilages surrounded by

terraced farmland, side-trip to cheese factory and monastery, unique mani walls and stupas

From Shivalaya the trail climbs steeply up the ridge to the scattered village of **Sangbadanda** with a schoolhouse (7350 feet, 2240 m) in **1¼–1¾ hours**, and a lodge and shops. Just up from the schoolhouse, the trail divides. The right branch continues to Kasourbas, another Sherpa settlement, and tea shops of Gatte Khola before reaching **Deurali** in **2 –2½ hours**.

Detour to Cheese Factory and Monastery from Sanbadanda to Deurali

Alternatively, a left branch from Sanbadanda heads up through Baldanda (no facilities), crossing a road and passing a serene meadow as you follow the ridgeline through dense rhododendron on a faint trail to the Swiss-designed cheese factory at **Thodung** (10,140 feet, 3091 m), about **2½ hours** from Sangbadanda.

Established in 1959 it was the second of its kind in Nepal, the first was built in the Langtang Region. Besides procuring a wedge of cheese, take in the view of Gauri-Shankar to the north. This twin-peaked mountain is named after the god couple, Parvati (aka, Gauri) and Shiva

(aka, Shankar). Although 5,500 ft (1700 m) lower than Everest, Gauri-Shankar at 23,406 feet, 7134 m, was once thought to be the highest peak in the world, simply because of its vibrant visibility from afar. There is an isolated monastery 30 minutes southwest of the cheese factory with 22 monks and 12 nuns in residence and an adjoining school for them. Visitors are welcome to the prayer ceremonies in the early morning (around 6 AM) and late afternoon (around 4:30 PM). The central figure in the meditation hall is known as Chenresig in Tibetan (aka, Avalokeshivara in Sanskrit) of whom the Dalai Lama is believed to be an emanation. Donations will go towards operation of the monastery and school.

From Thodung, follow south along the ridge to the pass - **Deurali** (8885 ft, 2708 m), in less than **1 hour**. Deurali has several choices for accommodation as well as a long series of *mani* walls (walls made of stones that have prayers chiseled into them) in parallel, quite a unique sight as often *mani* walls are solitary (one wall) and not arranged side-by-side like the several in unison here. Deurali also has a less well-known cheese factory with cheese produced mostly from cow's milk at the southeast of the saddle adjoining a lodge.

From Deurali pass, descend into the broad, fertile valley to the east. The trail passes lodges along the way down to two large *stupa* of a *gomba* (monastery) at the scattered village of **Bhandar** (7200 feet, 2194 m) in **1 hour**.

Although possible to reach Bhandar by vehicle depending on the season and condition of the road, the ride is grueling. The road is being pushed further to the next waypoint, Kinja and beyond. Bhandar's bus station lies at Bambti Bhandar, 20 minutes of level walk south of Bhandar. *Lonely Planet* likens Bambti Bhandar to 'the old west'. With wide, dusty avenues and wooden plank dwellings. It truly does have the feel of Laredo, a gunslinger's Nirvana, but don't expect shootouts here. TV antennas, vehicles and other sprinklings of modernity give away its yearnings for the modern era. The bus park is at the top of the settlement and if you choose vehicle travel as an option on the way out, be prepared for a long ordeal. Departure is early morning and arrival in Kathmandu reaches into the evening and passes through rugged sections of road.

Bhandar's monastery is called Changma Urgyen Choling and the five or so monks in residence follow the Nyingma lineage. Visitors are welcome for early morning and early evening prayer ceremonies. There are several cozy lodges near the monastery to spend the night.

DAY 3 – BHANDAR TO KINJA
Start: Bhandar 2194 m
End: Kinja 1634 m
Time: 3 hrs
Highlights: remote landscape, lush hills, valley views

Descend from Bhandar's fertile plateau to cross a stream and continue through scenic forests and terraced fields. You will find lodging and shops along the way as you contour above the Likhu Khola. Do not descend to the first suspension bridge seen below the trail. Continue up the valley to cross the river on a suspension bridge adjacent from Kinja. You then pass over another bridge to cross a tributary, the Kinja Khola, and through a welcome gateway painted with political slogans and on into the market area of Kinja. It takes **3 hours** from Bhandar to **Kinja** (5360 feet, 1634 m) with its numerous lodges and well-stocked shops.

DAY 4 – KINJA TO DAKCHU (OR KATHBISAUNE)
Start: Kinja 1634 m
End: Dakchu 2850 m
Time: 3¾–4½ hrs

17

Highlights: serene forests, cooler climate, isolated settings, distant mountain views

From Kinja, begin the climb to Lamjura La (11,580 feet, 3530 m), a lofty pass that will be the highest point of the journey to the Khumbu until Namche Bazaar, a week beyond. Ascend from the east end of Kinja's market area and follow a ridge more or less on the south side. Pass Septang with shops and then Chimbu (7168 feet, 2185m) with shops and a Danish-sponsored school and continue on to Nimur with an unmarked lodge and tea shop. Reach **Sete** (8450 feet, 2575 m), with several well-appointed lodges in **2¾–3½ hours** from Kinja. The trail continues along the ridge. Reach the few houses and six lodges of Dakchu (9350 feet, 2850 m) in **1 hour**. Just beyond, is Kathbisaune with a pleasant, solo lodge. Kathbisaune translates to 'wood resting place' and takes its name as a it was a place once well-known for porters to relieve their loads (often of building materials) and rest for a while.

DAY 5 – DAKCHU TO JUNBESI
Start: Dakchu 2850 m
End: Junbesi 2675 m
Time: 4¾–5¾ hrs
Highlights: mountain pass of Lamjura La (3530 m), serene forests, remote villages, terraced fields, Buddhist culture and monasteries of Junbesi

Ascend to **Goyem** (10,350 feet, 3155 m), **45 minutes** from Dakchu with a spread-out selection of tea shops and lodges and more lodging above in Kare. Beyond you will reach a lodge with a sign that indicates it is *at* Lamjura Pass although the actual pass is another hour away. Reach a cluster of lodges that is closer to Lamjura La but still 30 minutes from the pass itself. (A side-excursion trail to Pikey Peak 4,068 m with a sweeping, magnificent panorama branches away at these lodges). Continue through forested area and a *stupa* en route to **Lamjura La** (11,582 feet, 3530 m), **2¼–2¾ hours** from Dakchu with two lodges, each on either side of the pass.

The trail descends through a serene forest to Traktor, with three tranquil lodges (9380 feet, 2860 m) spread out 10 minutes from one another. Continue on the north side of the valley to a notch along a ridgeline and drop down to lively **Junbesi** (8775 feet, 2675 m) in **2½-3 hours** from the pass.

JUNBESI

Junbesi is an ideal place to take an extra day if time allows to rejuvenate and soak up the pastoral atmosphere and explore the Vajrayana Buddhist culture with several surrounding monasteries. Junbesi has many lodges to choose from, a visitor center and school built by Edmund Hillary's Himalayan Trust. There are at least five active monasteries in this area, including Serlo, perched above Junebesi to the west.

A **1¼-hour** walk from the main trail to the north of Junbesi is Thubten Chholing Gomba, an active monastery with associated nunnery and several hundred residents. The founder was the revered 31st Trulshik Rinpoche. He arrived in exile from Tibet's Rongbuk Monastery following the Chinese occupation there. The life of this *rinpoche* was the subject of a 1986 British documentary film entitled *Lord of the Dance, Destroyer of Illusion.* He passed away in September 2011. From this monastery, a high route continues to Dudh Kunda (Milk Lake), a lake in the lap of the mountains that is a popular destination during festival times. It lies in isolated highlands with no facilities and therefore, self-sufficiency is required to visit there.

DAY 6 - JUNBESI TO RINGMU
Start: Junbesi 2675 m
End: Ringmu 2720 m
Time: 4–4½+ hrs
Highlights: several route choices, serene forests and landscape, possible view of Everest, local fruits and locally brewed spirits

There are two main options to continue from Junbesi to Ringmu. The first is the usual way preferred by most travelers. The second option is slightly longer (while another option is arriving to Ringmo by vehicle by way of Salleri/Paphlu from Kathmandu, see **C1** and **C2** below).

A. Junbesi to Ringmu along the popular route

To continue on the usual route, then cross the Junbesi Khola on a bridge below the *stupa*. Stay to the left (to the right continues to Phaphlu which has road service to Kathmandu (as well as an airstrip) and Salleri, administrative headquarters of Solu–Khumbu District). Reach the lodges of Phurtyang (9975 feet, 3040 m), and look for sightings of distant Mount Everest if the weather is clear. Climb the ridge to the north for better views. Continue up the valley of the Dudhkunda (aka, Ringmo Khola) to the town of **Sallung** (9688 feet, 2953 m), with more lodges, **2½-3 hours** from Junbesi.

The trail descends across tributaries (one with a magnificent, stone-built cantilever bridge), and then the main river of the Dudhkunda. Ascend to a large *stupa* at **Ringmu** (8924 feet, 2720 m), **1½ hours** from Sallung. This attractive settlement has lodges and a health post. The *stupa* sits at a signed trail junction. The right branch heads south to to a road encroaching towards Ringmo from Phaphlu, a town with an airfield (see **C** below on hiking to Ringmu from Salleri/Paphlu to Ringmu).

B. Alternate Approach, Junbesi to Ringmu (or Paphlu) via Beni

This is a scenic, lesser-used alternative to the usual route to Ringmo described above, or if you are headed to the airport or road at Paphlu from Junbesi. Leaving Junbesi, after crossing the Junbesi Khola below the *stupa*, stay to the right and pass through Khunje with apple trees and then descend to **Najing** in **1¼ hours**. The trail splits here, right goes toward Lamjura La and out to Jiri; stay left to descend to the valley bottom and then cross over the Dudhkunda Khola on a suspension **bridge** in **45 minutes**. Nearby are a lodge, shop and school of Beni with a fine, grassy area near the river offering attractive camping possibilities. From the bridge, head left to climb through the forest above the river to idyllic **Lower Phera** in **30 minutes**. You might find fresh apples and plums here depending on the season. Continue to ascend with excellent views of Numbur (6958 m) and Khatang (6852 m) peaks to the **upper route** to Ringmu from Phaplu in **30-45 minutes**. **Ringmo** is another **1-1½ hours** contour north through pine and rhododendron forest (see below for description onward from Ringmu).

C. Walking in from Salleri/Paphlu to Ringmu

The road is being pushed ever further from Paphlu to Ringmu and before long will arrive at Ringmo village itself. Going by road saves time, but the grueling ride will test your physical and mental stamina. It is an uncomfortable, long haul from Kathmandu to Salleri, administrative headquarters of Solu-Khumbu district. The road journey in from Kathmandu will change with completion of a highway heading directly east from Kathmandu (after many years of construction and delays, it is nearing completion). Going the other direction, the journey from Salleri to Kathmandu is currently some 20 hours by jeep and approximately 3000 NRS/pax. Another option if a jeep isn't going all the way to

Kathmandu at the time you would like to go, is to travel by vehicle as far as the east-west highway in the southern plains and change vehicles there.

Salleri has a bustling bazaar and **tourist accommodation**. It is a **20-30 minute** walk up along the wide road from Salleri to Paphlu. The air strip lies at the north end of Paphlu (with views of Khatang peak to the north). The large hospital is above the airport and Paphlu offers many lodges for your choosing. A monastery is 10 minutes north at a trail junction. From this *gomba* the trail branches with the road to the right and a lower trail to the left that offers an alternate route to escape the roadway. This left, lower trail (**C1** below) heads down to the river at Beni and will be longer by about 30 minutes but more scenic than following the road (**C2** below).

C1. Lower Route Paphlu to Ringmu via Beni. The lower route is also along the route towards Junbesi by way of Beni. Descend, passing shops on the way to **Beni** in **1½-1¾ hours**. Beni has a lodge and shops as well as a secondary school. It lies at the junction of the Dudh Kunda Khola and the Basa Khola which join to form the Beni Khola at an area that offers alluring camping possibilities. Do not cross the Dudh Kunda Khola

but climb through the forest above the river to **Lower Phera** in **30 minutes**. You will find apples and plums here if the season is right. Continue to ascend with excellent views of Numbur (6958 m) and Khatang (6852 m) and tie in to the upper route from Phaplu in **30-45 minutes**. Ringmu is a further **1-1½ hours** contour north through pine and rhododendron (see the description below for traveling onward from Ringmu).

C2. Upper Route Paphlu to Ringmu. This route continues to the right from the *gomba* north of Paphlu airport and follows the roadway to Phera and eventually beyond to Ringmo. Pass through Cheuwang with a magnificent *gomba* perched high above in the bluffs, and Jongbuk to reach **Phera** in **2½ hours**. Contour north for **1½ hours** through a pine and rhododendron forest to **Ringmu**.

Ringmu (8924 feet, 2720 m). The homes of Ringmo are-surrounded by apple and apricot trees and locals make a refreshing *roxy* from these fruits; perhaps a glass will lift your spirit and rejuvenate tired muscles for the onward and upward journey.

DAY 7 - Ringmu to Nuntale
Start: Ringmu 2720 m
End: Nuntale 2245 m
Time: 2½-3 hrs
Highlights: Tragsindho La (3071 m), monastery and nunnery,

wide-open design of laid-back Nuntale

From Ringmu, the trail climbs a wide path to Pangoma with Gauri-Shankar Lodge and a tea shop where you can branch to the north (a remote several day traverse) to yak pastures and a high lake, Dudh Kunda (Milk Lake). Dudh Kunda is considered a holy lake and pilgrimage destination during festival times. To continue to the Khumbu, ascend to the right (east) through a forest to a clearing with a *mani* wall that surrounds an isolated, mysterious *stupa* that might seem more suited for the jungles of Cambodia. It covered in moss and has a unique shape not seen elsewhere in Nepal.

Continue steeply to **Tragsindho La** (10,075 feet, 3071 m) with a large white *stupa, mani* walls, prayer flags, and two lodges, **1-1¼ hours from Ringmu**. Enjoy views to the north with Numbur Peak particularly radiant. To the east beyond a *kani* gateway is the Dudh Kosi (Milk River) Valley which will be followed up to Namche Bazaar. Look for a view of Thamserku (21,713 ft/6618 m) after you pass through the gateway. Less than five minutes below is the large, majestic **Tragsindho Monastery** with nearby lodges and an adjoining nunnery and health clinic. If you

pay a visit at prayer time then you are in for a celestial experience of ritual chanting and symbolic music -- forget the cares and troubles of the world for a while.

The trail descends to the southeast, passes through forests, and emerges at the spacious settlement of **Nuntale** (Manidingma, 7365 feet, 2245 m) in **1½-1¾ hours**. Nuntale has a wide, stone avenue with many shops and lodges and a police check point where you might be asked to register your details.

DAY 8 – NUNTALE TO KARIKHOLA
Start: Nuntale 2245 m
End: Karikhola 2004 m
Time: 3¾–4¼ hrs
Highlights: terraced fields, rumbling Dudh Kosi (Milk River) in lush valley, pleasant villages

---

Descend steeply through terraced fields into oak forests to Juving Pul with tea shops near a bridge over the Dudh Kosi (4898 feet, 1493 m), **1½-2 hours** from Nuntale.

On the other side of the river, ascend to the left and follow up the valley through forest. Climb through terraces to reach a Rai village of **Juving** (5500 feet, 1676 m) in **45 minutes** with pleasant lodges. Rai are an indigenous clan in Nepal prominent in the UK's Gurkha Regiments. If you are up for something different, try a local beverage called *tongba* with the strength between beer and wine. It is a traditional Rai-Limbu (Limbu is another indigenous clan of Nepal) swill named after the large wooden vessel it comes in. The jug is filled to the brim with fermented millet and hot water is added over it. The alcohol seeps out from the millet, and the infusion is traditionally imbibed through a bamboo straw. A thermos of hot water is supplied and water is refilled as needed, the millet gradually loses alcoholic strength and is spent after about four to five refills.

Ascend to a prominent notch in the ridgeline with lodges and a newly built monastery Pema Namding Gomba of the Nyingma lineage (the prayer hall features a central figure of Guru Rinpoche flanked by Sakyamuni Buddha and Chenresig) overlooking the spread out village of **Karikhola** (6575 feet, 2004 m), **1½ hours** from Juving. It takes 30 minutes to walk from the notch at the upper end to the lower end of this scattered village with a police check post about midway. The upper end has a signed trail to Mera Peak via Pangkom village perched above to the east. A hospital and most of Karikhola's homes are above the trail with fields below. The town has lodges interspersed throughout and some well-stocked shops at the lower end if you need to re-supply with snacks and gear.

DAY 9 – KARIKHOLA TO POIYAN
Start: Karikhola 2004 m
End: Poiyan 2775 m
Time: 4¼-4¾– hrs
Highlights: tranquil forests, isolated villages, traditional lifestyles, monasteries

---

Descend to cross a bridge over the Kari Khola, and ascend to more lodging along a steep ascent to the cluster of pastel-painted lodges of **Bupsa, aka, Gomba Danda** (7700 feet, 2347 m), **1¼-1½ hours from the lower end of Karikhola.** A visit to the small, often unmanned *gomba* (built in 1892 and restored in 2003 with assistance from the Moving Mountains Trust, UK) can be arranged if you can find and coax the keyholder, one of the lodge owners, to open it. (A trail to the east leads to Kharte, Balukap and Pangkom on the trek towards the Arun Valley -- this strenuous journey crosses several magnificent and remote river valleys to Tumlingtar where auto and plane service is available for a return to Kathmandu.)

Pass shops and lodges on a grinding ascent to three more lodges of Kare and continue by more shops, restaurants and another lodge on the way up to the **Khari La** with teashops about an hour from Kare, **2-2¼ hours from Bupsa**. Look for snowy Cho Oyu from here; it ranks as the world's sixth highest peak and Gyachung Kang is visible, too. Continue along a tributary valley to the east (another trail to Pangkom branches steeply up to the right from the main trail) before crossing the Poiyan Khola in **30 minutes** from Khari La. In another **30 minutes** of ascent from the bridge reach **Poiyan**. The hamlet has a health post at the northwest end and spread-out accommodations with charming names like Beehive Lodge (with a little imagination, its stacked construction might resemble a honeycombed bee hive) and Apple Pie Lodge, **3–3½ hours from Bupsa.**

DAY 10 –POIYAN TO CHEPLUNG
Start: Poiyan 2775 m
End: Chelung 2680 m
Time: 3½-4+ hrs
Highlights: serene forests, traditional lifestyles, views of snowcapped Himalayan peaks, route choices -- mountain town of Lukla with airfield and hospital

---

Continue to climb through more lodges of Cheubas to round a ridge with another lodge at Chutok La and teashops at the crest of a ridge offering broad views. Descend to the lodge and tea shop of **Pakepani in an hour**. Descend to the lodges of Surkhe (7523 feet, 2293 m) on both sides of the **Surkhe Khola in under 1 hour from Pakepani, 2-2¼ hours from Poiyan.**

There are two options from Surkhe, a high route via Lukla and a more direct route to the Khumbu bypassing Lukla, outlined below as A and B.

Twenty minutes beyond Surkhe, a trail ascends to the right for Lukla. The mountain airstrip of Lukla is 2 hours from here. The easier, more direct route to the Khumbu bypasses Lukla and continues straight to Chaumrikharka. The trails tie in again at Cheplung to the north. The detour to Lukla is steep but the town is fascinating with many restaurants, pubs and bakeries and shops that cater to tourists where you can stock up for the days ahead or wait until Namche where goods are priced similarly and avoid the pack weight for another day or two.

A.   To   Cheplung   via Chaumrikarka bypassing Lukla
To continue straight to Cheplung, stay left and pass through Mushe before ascending to **Chaumrikharka** (also known as Dungde, 8900 feet, 2713 m), with lodges, **1½–1¾ hours** from Surkhe. Continue to **Cheplung** (8792 feet, 2680 m), a spread out village, in **20 minutes** from Chaumrikharka. The trail from Lukla ties in here, and if you

walked in from Jiri, Shivalaya, Bhandar or Phaplu, the changes in character of the trail will be obvious. It will now be busy with other travelers and more commercial facilities. Cheplang has several lodges and a small *gomba*, majestically set into the bluff above the village. See below for more information about this enchanting *gomba*.

B. To Cheplung via Lukla and Tenzing-Hillary Airport

20 **minutes** north of Surkhe, ascend along the trail branching to the right. The trail passes through isolated forest before arriving at the few houses of Hari Khola and then Tribeni Mahadev Shrine near the confluence of three small streams. Reach a quarry at the western end of the airstrip of Lukla in **2 hours** and the lively bazaar next to it.

LUKLA **(9350 feet, 2850 m)** Most people opt to fly into Lukla (9350 feet, 2850 m) rather than hike in from Jiri or the Arun Valley. Although arriving by plane saves time, acclimatization to altitude must be considered before ascending upward too quickly. Lukla is a major trekking center, with shops that sell and rent gear. In addition to an airstrip nestled among spectacular peaks, there are many lodges featuring food and accommodations of varying standards, banking, internet services, bakeries, bars, billiards and even a cinema hall. Most of these facilities are along the walkway running north from the airport (with some tourist facilities on the south side of the runway, too). There is now even a *Yakdonald's* and a coffee shop that has borrowed Starbucks famous brand name and has quite a broad menu of delights that would do the mother corporation proud.

Because of its airfield, Lukla is a major staging area for treks and helicopter excursions up to the Khumbu. The airstrip (9350 feet, 2850 m) was constructed in 1964 specifically to help shuttle building materials to Kunde Hospital above Namche and because of the airport, it has grown into a major tourist hub. Flights to Kathmandu can get backed up during the high season and especially if the weather obstructs visibility and flights are delayed. Confirm you flight out of Lukla as soon as you arrive and make sure to have a few buffer days for your international flight out of Nepal to allow flexibility should delays hit in Lukla. Kathmandu has plenty to explore if you arrive back there with extra time to spend. If you consider chartering a helicopter from Lukla to Kathmandu, the going rate is around $3000 USD (up to six people).

25

For people flying in, the runway at Lukla is built into a slope at an incline and as planes dip on the approach it can give the harrowing perception that the upcoming landing strip is perpendicular to the line of flight, quite an electrifying illusion.

Some guidebooks claim that the high-elevation landing strip built at an incline has not had a plane accident. As recently as both October 2008 and 2010, passenger planes crashed while landing. That said, Nepal has some of the best pilots in the world, skilled at flying in the Himalaya where 'the clouds have rocks in them'.

On a lighter note, if you are in Lukla on a Thursday, this weekly market day will provide a suitable distraction with traders arriving from the surrounding areas to sell and barter goods. The bazaar takes place below Lukla Resort at the northern edge of the airfield near a kerosene depot. At other times, these grounds double as a volleyball court for both locals and trekking staff with free time while in staging before or after a trek.

Lukla has a porter's clothing bank along the main avenue (supported by Porters Progress UK). Consider donating gear on your way out which porters in need can rent for free. The clothing bank is located on the second floor of the building across from the Scottish Pub and Everest Coffee Cafe.

The majority of the town's homes are below the main avenue as is Kemgon Thasi Choling Gomba with an adjoining German-sponsored thankga painting school. Further below to the west is a large, flat ground where riding bicycles has become popular. Cycles are rented for 50 NRS per 30 minutes.

Above the airstrip to the southeast (along the route that leads to Mera Peak) is Pasang Lhamu-Nicole Niquille Hospital opened with Swiss collaboration. Closed Saturday, hours are otherwise 9:30-4, Sunday-Thursday, 9:30-1 Friday. A post office is situated on the south side of the airport.

As a staging area, Lukla has many local restaurants catering to porters and trekking staff. These local establishments serve up cheap food and drinks, including local moonshine known as *roxy* and its less-refined, cheaper cousin, *chyang*, a sour alcoholic mash. These places are lively establishments but usually unmarked. Look for a thick cloth with Tibetan designs hanging over a doorway and be prepared for much attention if you patronize them. Not many foreigners seek these places out, and you will likely get the friendly but typical questions about who you are, which country you are from and the minutiae of your journey as well your life beyond Nepal. For short-term visitors this can be quite fun and flattering and a great way to make friends! *Cheers and salud!*

LUKLA TO CHEPLUNG

To proceed from Lukla toward the Khumbu, find two *kani* gateways at the north end of town, the second one is dedicated to Pasang Lhamu Sherpa, first Nepali women to summit Mt. Everest in April 1993 (she perished in an accident on the descent). A police post near the gateways might require you to register your passport (Sagarmatha National Park boundary is a half day away at Jorsale and entry permits are not required until Monjo, 3–4 hours from Lukla). Descend and contour above the scattered homes of Kengma. The *gomba* below and large school are considered to be part of Chaumrikarkha village rather than Kengma village. Another *gomba* lies out of sight from the trail below the shelf of land. Within **40 minutes from Lukla,** join the main trail from Jiri/Shivalaya at the spread out village of **Cheplung** (8840 feet, 2680 m) where there are lodges.

DAY 11 –CHEPLUNG TO NAMCHE BAZAAR
Start: Chelung 2680 m
End: Namche Bazaar 3446 m
Time: 5-6¼ hrs

Highlights: Samdenling Gomba, livelier trail, Sagamatha National Park entrance, historic settlement of Namche Bazaar—Gateway to the Khumbu, bakeries, nightlife

All trekkers heading to Khumbu, whether on foot from lower Solu or by plane to Lukla, will pass through Cheplung. If coming from Jiri you will notice from here onward that the route is much more structured for tourists compared to the quieter area on the way in. An international blend of travelers will be encountered at lodges, restaurants and along the trailways. These fellow mountain lovers from around the globe provide a forum for meeting and broad ranging conversations at lodges, tea shops, bakeries, bars and dining halls. Cultural differences may seem great but that does not mean they can't be bridged, at least over a meal and drink while mutually admiring the dazzling natural scenery.

Cheplung's **Samdenling Gomba** is elegantly built into the bluffs above the village. Should you wander up for a visit, inside you will find the figures of Guru Rinpoche (aka, Padmasambhava in Sansrkit), Gautam Buddha and Green Tara (aka, Pawa Chaey).

The village also has a colorful newer *gomba* along the trailside, a health post and police post. Above the police post is a Japanese established apple orchard. Across the Dudh Kosi Valley is the serene, untouched village of Sengma. Trekkers with time and inspiration can get off the beaten path and pay a visit to this serene hamlet away from the usual trekking highway.

The route onward from Cheplung follows north up the Dudh Kosi (Milk River) Valley to the Sagarmatha National Park's entry post at Monjo and beyond to the Khumbu region gateway of Namche Bazaar. Radiant, snowy mountains begin peering down from all angles as you make your way up the majestic valley.

To proceed from **Cheplung**, head north to several lodges at **Thado Kosi**, **30-45 minutes** from Cheplung. Cross the river on a steel box bridge (8380 feet, 2554 m) with a view to the east of the towering Kusum Kanguru (20,898 feet, 6370 m), a so-called 'trekking peak' (please see the MOUNTAINEERING section for more information on the Trekking Peaks of Nepal). The bustling settlement of **Ghat** (8350 feet, 2545 m) is another **20-30 minutes away**. Above the primary school, Ghat has a hillside filled with billowing prayer flags. Local Buddhists believe that the prayer flags send prayers written on them can reach intercessory deities with each flutter of the cloth and are of considerable merit for those who placed them there (and considered to be beneficial to all passersby, too). There are many lodges in this Ghat and a private *gomba* adjoins a hotel near the top, northern end where a shop sells filtered water using an on-site filter, a blessing to the environment compared to the usual bottled water on sale.

Proceed to **Phakding** (8700 feet, 2652 m), on both sides of the river, in 20 more minutes, **1¼-1¾ hours** from Cheplung. Phakding is commonly chosen as an overnight stopover for people who have flown into Lukla, and it is often crowded. Other lodging choices (there are many) along the way may be more attractive to avoid the mobs of people at popular waypoints. Cross to the west (right) bank (8600 feet, 2621 m) of the Dudh Kosi. Above on the wooded hillside lies Pema Choling Monastery. To reach it for a visit, take the left branch from the main trail at Zanfute, 10 minutes up the trail from Phakding, and ascend for 20-30 minutes to the *gomba*.

Side Trip to Pangjung. *This full-day hike to a viewpoint south of the park boundary offers* *astonishing views of Everest and surrounding, snowcapped titans. It is best to hire a local guide to show the way. The trail ascends from the west side of the river just to the north of **Phakding** at Zanphute and passes the village of Rimijung in 15-30 minutes with its associated Pemacholing Monastery (founded over 350 years ago according to locals). The nunnery at Gomlha is another 30-45 minutes beyond. The route then passes seasonal herders' huts along the way to **Panjung** which possibly has lodging (check locally that it is available before counting on it). The side-trip endeavor involves a climb of over 3300 feet (1000 m). Allow at least **3-4 hours each way**. This less-traveled trail might be an opportunity to get closer to nature and see rare wildlife in their natural environment compared to the main routes. Some of the mammals found within the region include Himalayan black bear, langur, marten, pika, weasel, jackal, and Himalayan mouse hare.*

On the main trail from Zanfute, and just beyond a tributary, climb through blue pine and rhododendron forests, past lodges and a few timber-built houses of a small settlement called Tok-Tok.

(A side trail ascends from Tok-Tok for a long, strenuous journey to Kongde, a jaw-dropping viewpoint with two luxury lodges. The isolated route follows the Bhote Kosi Valley to Thame in western Khumbu. This route will be outlined in reverse from Thame if you are looking for an adventure and wish to vary the return journey and prolong panoramas of the colossal Himalayan titans). Continue with views of Thamserku to the next settlement of **Benkar** (8875 feet, 2905 m) with lodges an **1 hour** from Phakding.

In a short while, cross to the east (left) bank and climb up through the hamlet of Chumowa surrounded by pine and pass a TIMS (Trekker Information Management System) card checkpoint.

Cross another tributary, the Kyangshar Khola (9098 feet, 2773 m), before climbing to the large village and comfortable lodges of **Monjo (9300 feet, 2835 m)** about **45 minutes from Benkar**. As an acclimatization side trip, consider an extra night in Monjo and ascend to the east to tranquil meadows above the village with advantageous views to reward the effort.

SAGARMATHA NATIONAL PARK (445 square miles, 1148 sq km)

The Khumbu region is encompassed by Sagarmatha National Park (established 1976), designated as a World Heritage Site (Natural) in 1979 (and Ramsar Site in 2007). Sagarmatha National Park is the third most visited area of Nepal after Chitwan National Park and the Annapurna Conservation Area. The acclaimed attractions are the majestic Himalaya with the highest peaks on the planet, lofty villages in mountain valleys graced by accompanying monasteries, and of course, the legendary inhabitants, the Sherpa. Roughly 7000 residents call the Khumbu their home. The national park is also home to wildlife of which Tibetan snow cocks, musk deer, Himalayan tahr and mouse hare are frequently seen but most other mountain dwelling fauna are elusive to the human eye (and camera lens).

The altitude of Sagarmatha National Park ranges from 2835 m/9300 ft at Monjo Village to 8848 m/29,031 ft at the frozen pinnacle of Everest. Average rainfall is 150 mm to 200 mm (6-8 inches) which arrives mainly in July and August. To the north of Sagarmatha National Park is the Tibetan Frontier and China's Qomolangma Nature Reserve and to the East is Nepal's Makalu-Barun Conservation Area.

Continuing from Monjo

At the north end of Monjo at a narrowing in the trail, reach the Sagarmatha (Everest) National Park compound and gateway and pay an entrance fee (3000 NRS) at the check post (with attached visitor center) if you have not already obtained a permit (a passport-sized photo will be requested). The trail descends through a cleft by the side of a massive boulder and crosses to the west (true right) bank of the Dudh Kosi on a suspension bridge to **Jorsale (9100 feet, 2774 m) in 15 minutes**. This is the last village before Namche Bazaar.

Continue briefly up the west bank from Jorsale through blue pine forests to a bridge that crosses again to the east (left) bank. The trail follows upriver and climbs steeply above the confluence of the Bhote Kosi from the west and the Dudh Kosi from the east and spans the gorge on a thrillingly high, hanging bridge.

The grinding climb of some 1900 feet (600 m) to Namche Bazaar ascends through pine. A little less than halfway up at the crest of a prow, an inspiring glimpse of Everest and its satellite peaks is revealed (weather permitting)! Continue through pine, to a police post and several lodges at a junction.

Both paths at the junction continue to Namche; the lower

honors you with a traditional entryway *kani*. **Namche Bazaar,** gateway village to the Khumbu, is **1¾–2½ hours from Jorsale.**

NAMCHE BAZAAR (11,306 feet, 3446 m)

Namche Bazaar is set in a magnificent natural arena enclosed by peaks to the south, west and east including a soaring Thamserku 6623 m/21,729 ft (east) and the Kongde massif (southwest). The town has over fifty hotels and serves as a restful hub for replenishing supplies and rejuvenating before and after deeper forays into the Himalayan highlands.

From this marvelously located town there are several trekking options to explore, listed below, including a visit to the lofty threshold of the mountaineering holy grail herself, *Chomolungma* (aka, *Sagarmatha*, Everest).

History

Namche Bazaar was once a nexus for trade from India and Nepal's lowlands to the Tibet Frontier. *Nauche* (the preferred Sherpa pronunciation for this town) served as a transition point for goods, mainly grain, fabric, vegetable dyes, tea, spices, sugar and tobacco from the south which were bartered for Tibetan salt, livestock, wool, silk, carpet, turquoise and even religious texts from the north. Prior to about 1905, the area was merely a place of storage of goods for traders from nearby Kunde and Khumjung in between seasonal travels to the Tibetan plateau over a snowbound pass called Nangpa La (18,753 feet, 5716 m) and the other direction, down into the lowlands. The flow of goods slowed considerably when lower-priced, iodized salt from India was introduced to Nepal and abruptly fell off after China gained control of Tibet in1950-51.

Facilities

As the administrative center for the Khumbu, Namche Bazaar has many officials and offices, including an army base, police post, government-run health post, post office, banks, and even ATM dispensers. Namche also has shops to buy and rent gear, and nowadays a few authentic outlet shops are in operation for premium clothing and kit. A modern dental clinic lies at the southeast side of town above a porter's shelter. Trekkers can avail themselves of services at reasonable prices. A health clinic lies along the northern edge of Namche below a blue pine nursery. The clinic is closed Saturday, otherwise, hours are daily 10-3 except Wednesday, 10-1.

With a growing number of tourist establishments including bars, billiard halls, bakeries, pharmacies, internet shops, and laundry service and much more, this well-supplied town can be a trekkers' paradise and a worthwhile place to explore and relax before and after going higher. Prices are *relatively* expensive, but a wide variety of practical goods are available with many souvenirs, too. Supplies and equipment from previous mountaineering expeditions can even be found in some of the trekking shops for purchase or rental.

Bakeries are especially popular hangouts for enjoying a hot drink and fresh pastry and meeting fellow tourists as are the modern pubs and eateries with names like Café 8848 (refers to the height of Everest and has plush seats with 1950's diner décor), Liquid Bar, Danfe Bar, and even the obligatory Irish Bar -- omnipresent throughout the globe's tourist hot spots. Most of the pubs have big screen televisions with the usual live sports, movies and fashion channel and many have a pool table, too, flown in by choppers. Save your thirst for alcoholic spirits for the return journey on the way back down the valley to lower elevations. Beer and booze are not beneficial for the acclimatization process and can do more harm than good, especially with increased demands that thinner air and oxygen places on the body and brain and an increased need for hydration at altitude.

Electricity in Namche and surrounding villages comes from a generating plant in the Thame valley that became operative in 1995 with Austrian assistance. Mobile phone service is available throughout much of the region to Namche Bazaar and beyond, and batteries can be charged in most places, given the right adapter (bring a universal adapter, or purchase a two-pin plug adapter found in Kathmandu.

The town's helipad lies along the first ridge to the southwest on the route to Thame. Namche is a well-appointed town, especially by Nepal standards, but despite the comforts, keep in mind the remoteness and high elevation of this area and surroundings. Although at a relatively low altitude compared to most of the Khumbu, acute mountain sickness (AMS) has been known to strike in Namche. Look after yourself and be aware of signs and symptoms in you travel mates (see **Staying Healthy** for more). Make sure you are adequately acclimatized before trekking higher.

If Namche is too glitzy for your liking, then Kunde, Khumjung, and Phortse are cozier. Another quieter option away from the hustle and bustle but close enough to avail yourself of Namche's many facilities and services is hidden Zarok (also spelled Jharok), with lodging and a few homes, 30 minutes up to the west from Namche's *gomba*.

What To Do In Namche

Visit the western side of Namche at sunset when the sky is drenched with color and peaks are aglow with rose, peach and purple hues.

The Sagarmatha National Park headquarters and information center above Namche on the ridge to the east (the area is referred to as Chorgang) is a great place to get to know the region. At the very least, you will be rewarded with impressive mountain views from this ridge top location, including Everest. The center has information boards with details about the history of the area and its people, flora and fauna, mountaineering and geology. It is closed Saturday and public holidays but otherwise open from 8 AM to 4 PM. In the area nearby the park headquarters is a Sherpa Cultural Museum and 'Everest Documentation Center' at a private, higher-end hotel. It features Everest's climbing history with an interesting section on climbers, too.

Namche's famous weekly market, held on Friday and Saturday at the southern end of town, is a lively affair. The weekly market is not of Sherpa origin but actually started in the 1960's by an Nepal Army officer stationed in Namche. It was established to meet the demands of an inflow of Nepali civil servants sent there when the *panchayat*, hierarchical system of governance, replaced a centuries old self-rule in the region. There is another daily market near the large *chorten* at the south end of Namche.

The lower, southern end of town has a series of water-driven prayer wheels where cobblers often set up along the wide path just above if you are in need of footwear repair wrought by the rugged trails. Nearby are unmarked restaurants similar to Lukla's with much cheaper food, patronized by the working crowd including porters and other staff. Look for a cloth hanging over the door with Tibetan motifs and be prepared for a lively atmosphere, and much attention with friendly questions.

An excellent day hike for acclimatization is to explore the crest of the ridge above Syangboche before descending to the prosperous Sherpa villages of Khumjung and Kunde (described below). Another idea is to head up the Thame valley as far as Thamo, 2-2¼ hours away, or all the way to Thame, childhood home of legendary Tenzing Norgay Sherpa, a 4-hour hike and spend a night there (the Namche to Thame route is described below).

Namche Gomba (locals refer to it as *Nauche Gonda*) lies just above the western edge of town and has an informative visitor center open from 8 AM to 5 PM (Sat 1-5 PM) with a break for lunch from 1-2 PM. The center provides details on the history of the area and its association to Buddhism and describes the meaning of many of the rituals and festivals of the region. **Dumchi** is the most prominent Sherpa festival, celebrated to strengthen ties in the community with group prayers and feasting, enlivened by drinking.

Sherpa generally follow the Nyingma tradition of Vajrayana Buddhism. The six primary lineages of modern Tibetan Buddhism include Nyingma, Sakya, Kagyu, Gelug, Jonang and Bon. (Bon is indigenous to Tibet and thought to predate Buddhism while some scholars now include it as one of the primary lineages of Tibetan Buddhism).

'Buddhism doesn't mean closing out the world; it means learning to embrace it with love and compassion.' -Tengboche **Visitor Center Placard**

Ecology in the Khumbu and destination of its rubbish

Namche is surrounded by nurseries above to the west, north and northeast. Most of the trees are swift-growing blue pine and the saplings are transplanted elsewhere in the Khumbu as part of reforestation efforts for depleted juniper and other firewood fuels.

Rubbish left behind by trekkers and climbers is likely to be burned or pitched into out of way locations or tossed into waterways, with an 'out of sight, out of mind' attitude that is common regarding garbage in Nepal. The Sagarmatha Pollution Control Committee (SPCC) is working hard to change this attitude and to keep the trails litter-free. They have set up disposal bins and maintain records of the weight of rubbish collected in the Namche area over the course of a year. Most of what is collected is incinerated just outside the town. For 2010/11, 54,295 kg of rubbish labeled as 'Paper/Plastic' (considered *burnable* despite the acrid, noxious fumes emitted by burned plastic) was collected and 8,779 kg of

'Can/glass/bottle/metallic   waste'   (*non-burnable*). For the three fiscal years of 2008/09-2010-2011, the SPCC burned 53,712 kg of garbage brought to Namche by expedition teams and recorded 15,067 batteries and 4,297 empty oxygen cylinders among other disposed items that were sent to Kathmandu.

For the so called 'Trekking Peaks' in the region over these three years, 9,084 kg of garbage was brought to Namche and Lukla for incineration and 11,200 cans among other refuse was sent to Kathmandu (which has its own severe waste disposal problems; the two formerly sacred rivers that run though Kathmandu have become dump sites and are generally open sewers in need of resuscitation).

MANI RIMDU

Mani Rimdu is a Sherpa-Buddhist and cultural festival unique to the Khumbu region. The name '*mani*' translates to jewel or gem and is part of Chenrezig's mantra, *Om Mani Padmi Hum* (please see below). '*Rimdu*' refers to the small maroon pills that are blessed during the ceremony and handed out to onlookers. The Mani Rimdu celebration has origins in Tibet, particularly Rongbuk Monastery. It was developed by Dzatzul Ngawang Tenzin Norbu, an avatar of Lama Sangwa Dorje, the lama who introduced Buddhism to the Khumbu.

Mani Rimdu is held annually at Tengboche and Chiwong monasteries between late October to November and sometimes early December and at Thame Gomba each May. The festival lasts two weeks (the final 3-4 days is when the public gets involved) and includes prayers and rituals, lively mask dancing, singing and blessings.

The festival begins with the creation of a sand mandala using topsoil brought in from a sacred place in the surrounding mountains. The mandala is completed in four days and becomes a focal point for daily prayers and rituals.

The most auspicious time for the local people is toward the end of the festival, the third to the last day referred to as *Om Tapne*. At this time, the *rinpoche* offers small, consecrated beads (known as Precious Pills) with blessings to the people. These pills are later ingested as needed and considered to be for protection and general well-being, a type of spiritual medicine.

The following day, the second to last, a large crowd attends monk dances. These melodramatic presentations take place in the monastery courtyard (fees are charged for foreign visitors). There are sixteen performances in all with monks dressed in grand costumes and wearing large masks that depict fierce-looking (but compassionate) deities. The show symbolizes the arrival of Guru Rinpoche (aka, *Padmasambhava* in Sanskrit) to Tibet in the 13th century C.E. Guru Rinpoche is also referred to as the Second Buddha by Vajrayana Buddhists. He introduced Buddhism from India to Tibet where it mixed with indigenous beliefs and the fascinating result is Tibetan Buddhism. The long performances depict the meaning of this style of Buddhism and the conquering of demons that represent primary obstacles to understanding and practicing *dharma* (*dharma* -- the instructions of Buddha regarding universal truth and the practice of those teachings). The main obstacles to successfully practicing *dharma* are ignorance, hatred, lust and greed.

Simple snacks and tea are served free of cost during the performances, and comic relief involves audience participation and a tendency toward slapstick humor and human bodily functions. Towards the end of the show, monks perform daredevil feats with a sword that elicits exuberant response from the excited crowd. Reactions include tossing to money, silk scarves and biscuits (cookies) into the courtyard for the monks to gather up as rewards.

Performances last into the early evening. Later, the monastery courtyard is filled with locals who sing and dance together for hours. The final day of the Mani Rimdu festival involves a fire ceremony performed by monks to symbolically purify the world of wrongdoing and harm. Then, the sand mandala is undone with the blessing that all beings find freedom from suffering. Mani Rimdu is a captivating festival for locals and visitors alike!

OM MANI PADMI HUM

The mantra of Chenresig, (aka, Avalokiteshevara in Sanskrit)-- the Dalai Lama is believed to be an avatar of Chenresig. This mantra is found inscribed (written, painted, etched) nearly everywhere in the Khumbu, that is, everywhere that humans can reach including prayer flags placed at the top of summits, festooning mountain passes and adorning bridges in valley basins. The script of the mantra is chiseled into *mani* stones that are placed into walls or heaped in mounds around settlements and along travel routes.

The translation is '*blessed be the jewel in the lotus*'. Interpretations vary as to the meaning, including '*enlightenment (the jewel) is here, right here on earth, in front of us (in the lotus)*'. Another variation is that the teachings of the Buddha (i.e., the jewel) will transform us into a lotus (a symbol of enlightenment-- growing from mud and murky water to blossoming in the sunlight above the dark water).

The mantra and other mantras and prayers are written on *lungta*, the Tibetan word for prayer flag. The name translates to 'wind horse' and *lungta* are believed to send prayers written on them to intercessory deities with each flutter of the fabric. These flags are of Tibetan origin and come in five primary colors. Blue represents space, white - water, red - fire, green - wood, and yellow - metal.

EIGHT SACRED SYMBOLS OF TIBETAN BUDDHISM

Known as *tashi tagya* in Tibetan and *ashtamanga* in Sanskrit, these designs are seen around Tibetan-origin populations and throughout the highland populations of Nepal. They are commonly found on *chorten, stupa* and *mani* stones and in paintings, textiles, ritual objects and inscriptions at homes, monasteries, restaurants and shops and even on tableware and everyday practical objects. The symbols are considered signs of good fortune, protection and well-being. Each motif has different meanings that are open to interpretation and the following is a brief summary of the significance of each symbol:

-**Eternal Knot** -- represents unity of the cosmos and time's endlessness as well as the union between wisdom and compassion, intention and action

-**Lotus** -- wholesome deeds rising from the coarse mud under murky waters – it grows and blossoms in the clear light of day; represents the process of enlightenment

-**Victory Banner** -- stands for the victory of wisdom over ignorance

-**Wheel of Dharma** -- the precious Buddhist teachings, especially the Eightfold Path and the Four Noble Truths

-**Vase** -- holds the waters of eternity and jewels of enlightenment

-**Pair of Golden Fish** -- swimming freely without fear of drowning in the waters of *Samsara* (worldly life)

-**Umbrella** -- protection from negative influences and suffering

-**Conch Shell** -- heralds the Buddha's teachings; signals group prayer time

COMPASSION 101

In monasteries and shrines you might notice water offerings in small goblets at an altar, along mantles of prayer halls, near statues and at the base of *thangka* and especially near images of *rinpoche*. The water is changed daily, sometimes twice or more. It is not simply an offering but an exercise for the giver. It is considered a training in compassion for transforming the mind. Water is relatively easy to obtain and provide and typically costs the giver nothing. The notion is that by providing something free, i.e., water, as a 'donation', resistance to giving in general is ultimately lessened. A person eventually develops a habit of giving without reluctance, and the ability to share more and more with others.

"If people knew the results of giving and sharing ... Even if it were their last bite, their last mouthful, they would not eat without having shared, if there were some being to receive their gift." - Sakyamuni Buddha (born in Nepal's Lumbini), Itivuttaka Sutta

THE SHERPA

The name Sherpa translates to *Sher*=east and *pa*=person -- in other words, 'easterner'. The east refers to eastern Tibet from where the people who bear the name Sherpa originally emigrated to Solu-Khumbu. They first arrived in the 1700s C.E. Sherpa have retained many Tibetan traits and ties with their Tibet roots, from traditional dress, language and customs to the Nyingma style of Vajrayana Buddhism (the lineage of the 'ancient ones'). Some scholars believe that Sherpa began to arrive in the Khumbu around 400 years ago. It is estimated that around 7000 live in the area but exodus to Kathmandu and beyond is taking its toll on the local population of the highlands.

The remote valleys of the Khumbu were once thought to have been uninhabited before the Sherpa arrived but research indicates that the area may have been inhabited long before the Sherpa arrival in the 18th century including evidence that the remote valleys were seasonally visited by Rai shepherds with livestock.

Nowadays, during Nepal's monsoon from June through September, resident Sherpa are busy pasturing livestock in the highlands above the settlements while closer to home, a single growing season provides a chance to sow and reap crops. They mostly raise potatoes in the Khumbu, which were first introduced in the 1800s. In fact, up to 90% of the crops in the Khumbu are potatoes. Fields are usually enclosed by stone walls to prevent animals from entering and to delineate separately owned tracts of land. Sherpa also cultivate barley and buckwheat, used for a traditional nutriment called *tsampa*, flour mixed with hot water or *solja*, a salt-butter tea, eaten as a doughy paste with perhaps a side dish of lentil soup or vegetables.

Traditional Sherpa dwellings are typically built of stone and mud with slate roofs or wood plank roofing secured by heavy stones (with increased wealth, tin has become popular). The front faces south and east to maximize exposure to sunlight and warmth. The ground floor is typically for storage, mostly firewood, and housing livestock. It is connected to living quarters above by an internal set of stairs. These internal stairs allow inhabitants to take care of animals and replenish fuel for fires without venturing outside. Additionally, heat generated from this ground-floor cellar radiates to the living quarters above, vital in the freezing winters.

Since the 1950s when westerners first visited the Khumbu, tourism has grown to a major source of income with a resultant growth of hotels, restaurants and shops in formerly traditional areas. This influx of visitors at first led to overharvesting of juniper, poached by the lodges, restaurants, and trekking companies as more fuel was needed. Juniper helps cohesion of the fragile, highland topsoil and harvesting it aggravated landscape erosion. At high elevations, juniper grows much too slowly to be sustainably harvested. Livestock droppings, a plentiful natural source of fuel, have supplemented the supply of fuel as has introduction of hydropower plants and solar panels. Nowadays, blue pine from nurseries surrounding Namche are being sourced to reforest the greater Khumbu.

Astrology and the lunar calendar play important roles in the Sherpa calendar, determining when to schedule important events and activities. **Dumje** is one of the most important Sherpa festivals and occurs toward the beginning of the monsoon, usually in late June or early July. The festival celebrates Sherpa community ties with group ceremonies, prayers, and banquets, spiced-up with locally brewed spirits.

Sherpa names commonly reveal the day of the week on which a child was born.

Nyima – Sunday
Dawa -- Monday
Mingma -- Tuesday
Lhakpa – Wednesday
Phurbu – Thursday
Pasang – Friday
Pemba -- Saturday.

Funeral rites for a deceased person last 49 days, an interval appropriate for the deceased to have determined a next incarnation. A long line of guests will visit the home of the deceased and much money is spent on this occasion to welcome and feed them.

Samsara is considered to be the relentless flow of change exemplified by birth, death and rebirth. An integral component of this continual rotation is *karma* (action), simply put, current circumstances are conditioned by previous actions. Rather than a higher being meting out punishment and reward, *karma* might be considered a universal principle such as a spiritual version of Newton's 3rd Law of Motion, "To every action there is always an equal and opposite reaction". *Karma* is simply a belief in cause and effect, from every action there is a result.

"After all, it is no more surprising to be born twice, than it is to be born once" –Voltaire.

NAMCHE'S NEARBY VILLAGES OF KHUMJUNG AND KUNDE BY WAY OF SYANGBOCHE

The airfield above Namche, known as **Syangboche** (12,205 feet, 3720 m) with a few nearby lodges, lies on a small plateau less than a **1 hour** hike above **Namche**. Reach it by following the trail that climbs up from the *gomba* on the west side of Namche. Another option is to ascend from the health clinic at the northern edge of town. It is a steep ascent to the northwest end of Syangboche airfield, now a helicopter landing site. Fixed-winged craft no longer operate here.

Follow the trail onward from the northwest end of the airstrip. In less than five minutes up the trail, it diverges near a Sagarmatha National Park building and relay towers with signs pointing the

way onward. For Kunde, stay left and proceed past a yak preserve run by Nepal's Ministry of Agriculture (additional grazing sites are near Pheriche and Pangboche). Male calves born at the preserve are sold to local farmers for 2000 NRS. Naks (female yaks) produce little milk but the quality is good (~13% fat). Naks yield around 600 ml/day but only lactate 2½ months in a year (July to mid-September). The female crossbreed between yaks and cows is called *zom* or *chaumri*. They are comparatively much more productive with slightly less quality of milk. The male crossbreed is called *zopke*.

From the yak preserve, climb to a crest (12,700 feet, 3871 m) in a peaceful juniper forest, then descend stairs to **Kunde** (12,602 feet, 3841 m) with a welcome gateway and lodges in **30-40 minutes** from **Syangboche**. The north end of this town is the site of locally staffed, well-equipped Kunde Hospital, built by Hillary's Himalayan Trust. The price for a consultation is 20 NRS for Nepalis and $50 USD for foreigners. *Himalayan Hospital* by Mike Gill provides Interesting background reading on the formation of Kunde Hospital.

You might notice that dwellings in Kunde and its sister settlement Khumjung all have the same color pattern, white-gray walls and green roofing (except for the monasteries). This is an attempt for the architecture to blend in with the natural landscape of the area.

Consider a side trip to the *gomba* and the crest of the ridge above it overlooking Kunde. Khumbu's protector deity is *Khumbila* (also, *Khumbi-Yul-Lha)*, and resides on the peak above town to the immediate north. This peak is sacred and off limits for climbing.

To reach **Khumjung**, the sister village of Kunde, you can follow east from **Kunde** for **10 minutes** or traverse directly from the trail at the northwest end of

Syangboche airfield. From Syangboche, take the trail heading right from the sign-posted junction near the National Park office and relay towers less than **five minutes** above the **airfield**. The sign indicates right to Khumjung and even advertises the fabled 'yeti scull' which will be found locked away in a cabinet inside Khumjung's monastery (find the monastery 'konyer' or keyholder and view the relic for a 'donation'). Savvy observers might find a peculiar resemblance between the scalp on display and that of the Himalayan serow, thought by some to be the likely creature that is mistaken for the *yeti.*)

Pass a large *chorten* and *mani* wall in a blue pine grove with thrilling mountain views including Everest and Ama Dablam. Descend through a welcome *kani* to a Himalayan Trust school and the lodges of **Khumjung** (12,400 feet, 3780 m) in **30–40 minutes** from Syangboche. The village *gomba* is set in a stand of trees to the north with the 'yeti scull' under lock and key in a cabinet inside the main prayer hall.

THE YETI MYSTERY UNFOLDS

Sherpa folklore describes *yetis* as shaggy critters with conical heads, pointed ears, and herculean strength -- enough to carry off husky yaks upon which they feast. *Yetis* are reputed to reach heights, head to toe, of up to a staggering 8 feet (2.44 m), and they haunt the most remote regions of the Himalaya, only rarely bringing trouble to inhabited settlements.

Sherpa believe in three types of *yeti*: **Drema** -- messenger of misfortune, **Chuti** -- preys on livestock, and **Midre** -- attacks all animals, including the human beast.

The celebrated *yeti* scalp and hand bones had long been kept at Khumjung Monastery (viewable for a 'donation'). Now, only the scalp remains. The late Sir Edmund Percival Hillary took the specimens on a tour outside Nepal in the 1960's. His attempt to verify this 'anomalous primate' did not meet with the same success as his mountaineering exploits. Science was unable to back him and authenticate a *yeti*.

Another mountaineering luminary, Reinhold Messner, was fascinated by the mystery after encountering a *yeti*-like creature in Eastern Tibet. He wrote a book on his personal search for *yeti* in the Himalaya (*My Quest for the Yeti: The World's Greatest Mountain Climber Confronts the Himalayas' Deepest Mystery,* St. Martin's Press, April 2000*)*.

Other expeditions have tried without fruition to find this animal whose existence has been based on anecdotal reports but not scientific corroboration. Messner eventually concluded (after an 11-year search) it was a type of bear...his search now seems to have come full circle with a recent genetic study out of Oxford University (published this July in the *Proceedings Of The Royal Society B: Biological Sciences*). Researchers matched DNA from hair samples found in the Himalaya with a prehistoric bear from The Pleistocene Epoch, roughly 2,500,000 to 11,500 years ago.

The search continues for a live specimen and *yeti* remains an eminent figure of cryptozoology. As a pop-culture icon, the name *yeti* surfaces not infrequently in the media and is used to promote everything from mountain bikes to pubs, banks, spas, hotels, bakeries, a golf course and much more. The *yeti* legend has beguiled the human race from the Himalaya to around the globe!

ONWARD FROM KHUMJUNG

Khumjung to Gokyo or Tengboche

To head to Tengboche or Gokyo, follow the trail out of the eastern end of Khumjung village. The path branches to the left toward Mong Danda and the Gokyo lakes or continues straight to head downhill to Sangnasa and Tengboche -- after 15-20 minutes of descent, the trail ties in to the direct trail from **Namche to Tengboche**. This junction is a minute before Sangnasa and about five minutes north of Kyangjuma. A signboard here indicates directions to Namche, Khumjung, Gokyo and Tengboche (*Note*: if you are heading to Gokyo from Khumjung, it would be better to take the trail branching left at the eastern edge of Khumjung, please see below).

Khumjung to Gokyo. To head toward Mong Danda and Gokyo stay left out of the eastern end of Khumjung. In less than 30 minutes, avoid a trail that branches to the left which is a very steep shortcut that is to be avoided unless you enjoy near-vertical trails! Instead, continue to cross a ridge and contour up to Mong Danda in **1¼-1½ hours** from Khumjung. (See the description from **NAMCHE TO GOKYO** for continuing from Mong Danda).

Khumjung to Namche. If heading back to Namche from Khumjung, one option is to climb up toward the swanky Everest View Hotel from the eastern end of Khumjung. Along the way, a ten minutes climb from Khumjung to the south will bring you to the Hillary Memorial Stupa built in honor of Sir Edmund, a man beloved by the local Sherpa community, especially for his mission to bring education, health care and air transport to the region. The Everest View Hotel is 30 minutes beyond the memorial. This posh hotel was built in 1974 and is situated on a crest (12,700 feet, 3870 m) with privileged views of Everest and much more. It is patronized by mostly Japanese clientele and the interior is decorated in Japanese style. Customers fly into Lukla and often continue by helicopter to Syangboche. Clearly, there are dangers of acute mountain sickness with a rapid ascent and oxygen is provided at the hotel for $20 USD/hour. Rooms go for $100-plus per night. Stop in for a hot drink at the beautifully set bar with impressive views north of the Himalaya in the hotel's luxuriant, charming setting. Coffee and tea prices are remarkably comparable to Namche lodges.

Descend past a lodge and another fancy hotel on a desolate trail to the western end of Syangboche airstrip and continue down to Chorgang in 30-45 minutes. Namche is 10 minutes downhill from Chorgang.

NAMCHE TO THAME

Most tourists who visit Thame do not stay the night, which can make it even more attractive for those who overnight there and wish to escape the crowds. Thame is about 1000 feet (300 m) higher than Namche, and therefore, it can be a useful stopover for acclimatization to altitude. The trail from **Namche** leads west from the *gomba* to round a ridge with a helipad in 10-15 minutes.

Contour through forest, and within 30 minutes, a direct trail from Syangboche ties in from above. Reach a large *stupa* at **Furte** (11,155 feet, 3400 m), with tea shops, and two lodges, as well as a government run tree nursery in 15 more minutes, **1-1¼ hours** from Namche.

Continue to Samsing with two tea shops and then reach Theso with an ancient looking *stupa* and *kani* gateway. Two trails to Mende and Lawudo Gomba ascend just out of Tesho, the second one with inviting stone steps, but stay left at that junction if you are on the way to **Thamo** (11,319 feet, 3450 m), reached in **20 minutes** from Tesho, **45 minutes–1 hour** from Furte.

Side Trip to Mende and Lawudo Monastery (and on to Samde for an alternate route to/from Thame). The houses of Mende are above to the north between Theso and Thamo. Above Mende is the monastery Lawudo Gomba. Monks and foreigners affiliated with Kopan Monastery in Kathmandu often take retreat there. Mende village itself has the luxury Everest Summit Lodge, affiliated with Intec, a German organization (other associated luxury accommodations are found in Trashinga, Lukla, Monjo, and Pangboche). Set menu prices at this full service lodge include $22

USD for dinner, $18 USD for lunch and $15 USD for breakfast.

Above, Lawudo Gomba has guest rooms for 1600 NRS per night including meals. The monastery is situated in a commanding location with an extensive panorama overlooking the valley. A few monks, nuns and attendants are in permanent residence. The nun who oversees the monastery is the elder sister of well-known Lama Zopa Rinpoche, abbot of Kopan Monastery, and their family hails from the surrounding area. The central figure inside the main prayer hall is *Chenrezig* (aka, *Avalokiteswara*), flanked on one side by Sakyamuni Buddha and the other side by Guru Rinpoche (aka, *Padmasambhava*) and Green Tara.

A 30 minute ascent to the west of the monastery is Cherok, an otherworldly retreat location built under an overhanging rock. There are isolated meditation huts built into the walls and crevices of the surrounding bluffs. Legend has it that Guru Rinpoche (aka, *Padmasambhava*) meditated here on his way to Tibet.

A direct trail from the *gomba* to Samde on the route to Thame follows west from Lawudo Gomba to Geduk where there is a dwelling before reaching Samde in **1½ hours**. Along the way, between Samde and Lawudo

Gomba and Mende look for the gorgeous, iridescent national bird of Nepal, the Impeyan pheasant (*Danfe* in Nepali), plentiful in this area but skittish and wary of approach.

Thamo to Thame

Thamo is location of the headquarters of a 630-kilowatt power project built with Austrian assistance. It began functioning in 1995 and electrifies the western section of the Khumbu. Most of the distribution lines are buried underground and do not disturb views!

Leaving Thamo, do not descend to the left to the river but climb past the village's newly refurbished monastery, with some 30 nuns and a few monks, at the top end of the village. Ascend to **Samde** (11,844 feet, 3610 m) in **30 minutes**, with two lodges and tea shops and a sweeping vantage of the distinctive Kwangde peaks. (The path from Mende and Lawudo Gomba joins here, offering an enticing, alternate return route on the way from Thame to Namche). The trail continues above the river before descending to a crossing alongside a canyon wall with large murals of three Buddhist saints. From left to right, Green Tara, Guru Rinpoche (aka, *Padmasambhava*) and Thang Teng Gampo watch over the trail and convey blessings to passersby. Cross the box bridge above the tumultuous Bhote Kosi roaring through a narrowing of the canyon walls. Ascend steeply, passing a *kani* entrance to **Thame** (12,400 feet, 3780 m), with seven lodges, in **¾-1 hour** from Samde, **1½ hours** from Thamo.

Above the hamlet, a dramatically perched monastery (12,925 feet, 3940 m) is set into the cliff face. The May occurrence of *Mani Rimdu* festival takes place here. A tea shop and guest house adjoin the monastery. For people with the time and energy, high above is Sundar viewpoint, a long day trip, and according to locals, more than 80 peaks can be viewed, including the Top of the World, Everest.

Thame Teng is the small settlement beyond the ridge to the north of Thame, and a rock climbing route has been established above the *chorten* to the east. Farther north up the Bhote Kosi lies the snowbound Nangpa La (18,753 feet, 5716 m), an important passage into Tibet. It was once the high point of a popular trading route that started in the 18th century. Nowadays, the Nangpa La serves as an entry point for Tibetan refugees escaping for political and religious reasons. A route to Gokyo follows this old route to Lungdhe Village before branching east to cross the high mountain pass Renjo La. However, for acclimatization purposes it is better to cross from the Gokyo side (described below in the section on Gokyo).

The Thame Khola (aka,Thengpo Khola) flows in from the west from the head of the valley where lies the Trashi Labsta, a challenging high pass (18,882 feet, 5755 m) leading to the remote Rolwaling Valley. This route requires ropes, ice axe, technical know-how, camping gear and an experienced guide.

Another exploration option in Thame is *The Thame Cultural Trail, 'The Heart of Thame Valley'*. This half day hike to raise cultural and ecological awareness includes fourteen 'rest points' with informative signs on the history, geography, culture and flora of the area. The trail starts at Thame School created in 1963 by the late Sir Edmund Hillary's Himalayan Trust Association nearby a Health Post.

The Thame Cultural Trail

Rest Point 1 The School in Thame
Rest Point 2 The Mill
Rest Point 3 Juniperus Recurva
Rest Point 4 Mani
Rest Point 5 Geomorphology of the Valley
Rest Point 6 Towards Nangpa La
Rest Point 7 Chorten, Stupa
Rest Point 8 Water Source and Large Mani
Rest Point 9 Domang
Rest Point 10 Birch (Takpa) Kyaro Gomba (Kyabrog Gomba)
Rest Point 11 Dry Stone Walling
Rest Point 12 Juniperus Indica (Phom)
Rest Point 13 View of Thame, Chorten Chhulung and Lung Ta, Kani
Rest Point 14 Om Mani Padme Hum, Thame Monastery

RETURN FROM THAME
Options for the return from Thame to Namche Bazaar include the following:

A. Retrace your footsteps back along the same way that you arrived

B. Visit the Powerhouse on an alternate return to Thamo: follow a trail from the southeast end of Thame village and cross over the Thame Khola. The trail passes the small, hydropower collection reservoir and branches left to surmount a fence on a small metal ladder in five minutes from the bridge. Descend through a nursery to the powerhouse near a bridge over the Bhote Kosi in 45 minutes. (From the powerhouse, a trail stays on the south side of the Bhote Kosi and ascends over a difficult, isolated route to the expensive lodging at Kongde before descending to Tok-Tok on the main route between Lukla and Namche. This long route is described next as **THAME TO TOK-TOK VIA KONGDE**).

Cross the Bhote Kosi, and ascend to Thamo in 30-45 mins where you meet the earlier route from Namche to Thame.

(Another trail from Thame to the powerhouse heads to the right a few minutes after descending through the *kani* gateway at the eastern end of Thame. This option will add a needless uphill section to the above described route).
C. Visit Mende and Lawudo Gomba: Return from Thame to Samde and from there, ascend to Mende, reached in 1½ hours before descending to Tesho and on to Namche (described above in reverse, see **Side Trip to Mende and Lawudo Monastery)**.

THAME TO TOK-TOK VIA KONGDE. Some trekkers refer to this route as a **Fourth Pass of the famed Three Passes**. **Advisory:** This is a long, isolated route with steep, exposed sections that have fixed lines in place. It should not be attempted without a guide unless you are fit and capable for a long day's hike and confident on exposed rock and sometimes ice. It lies mostly along the southern slope (facing north) of the Bhote Kosi Valley and therefore, receives relatively less sunshine. Snow and ice can build up along the trail and should be expected – do not attempt the route after fresh snowfall. Again, this is a strenuous journey that is not frequented by locals or other travelers (except for expensive guided trips). Bring rations with you as the only facilities along the way are two luxury hotels situated at 4200 m reached in **6-6½ hours** from Thame after a 600 m ascent and the next facilities thereafter are a 1500 m descent, **2½-2¾ hours** from the expensive, luxury hotels.

Begin from Thame at the trail from the southeast end of the village and cross over the Thame Khola. The trail passes the small, hydropower collection reservoir and branches left to cross over a fence on a small metal ladder in five minutes from the bridge. Descend through a nursery to the powerhouse in **45 minutes**. Pass over an outlet stream from the powerhouse, but do not cross the Bhote Kosi to the north. Instead, stay right to cross a tributary and ascend over a ridge to the west. Pass above the seasonal pasture area of Pare in **30 minutes**.

Continue to contour through rhododendron and then birch and begin to ascend steeply (across the valley from Thamo). Climb through a mixture of rhododendron, birch, bamboo, fir and juniper in a serene forest. Savor the tranquility on this trail 'far from the madding crowd', especially compared to the Everest Base Camp route. Reach a narrow valley in **2½ hours** from Pare and head up it to the south for **45 minutes** along the western slope. Reach a frosty stream and pass over it to the east. Ascend through a very steep section that is sometimes exposed and might have icy sections. Fixed lines and railings have been put in place but use caution as they might not be reliable and are rickety and not in the best condition. Contour west to two ritzy hotels on a windy ridge top known as Kongde, reached in **1½-2 more hours**. Yeti

Mountain Home is a chain of luxury accommodations (also found in Lukla, Phakding, Monjo, Namche and Thame). The location has splendid views from Thamserku to Everest. Food at the hotel is according to a set menu and rooms go for $120 USD/night including meals. If food is necessary, the adjacent Kongde Hotel is a better chance, as it has individual menu items for food and drinks although rooms go for $110 USD/night. To the west of the hotels is Sherpa Peak and south is Farapka Peak. Both viewpoints are at approximately 4600 m/15,100 ft and will improve an already staggering panorama of snowy peaks and highland valleys.

Descend to the west for **45 minutes** before heading south along the Dudh Kosi Valley to reach Tok-Tok in an additional **1¾-2 hours** (**2½-2¾ hours** from the Kongde hotels), near the bridge crossing to Zanfute.

UPPER KHUMBU AND THE THREE PASSES

The exhilarating Khumbu region has four main river valleys to explore, all surrounded majestically by soaring peaks, the highest in the world. From east to west the river valleys are the following:

-**Imja Khola** - Chukhung is the uppermost outpost en route to Island Peak

-**Khumbu Khola** - Gorak Shep is the uppermost settlement on the way to Everest Base Camp

-**Dudh Kosi** - Gokyo is the uppermost settlement next to Gokyo's 3rd lake

-**Bhote Kosi** - north of Thame, Lungdhe and Ariye are the uppermost settlements en route to the Renjo La.

Facilities exist within each valley, and they are interlinked by three high passes. East to West, the passes are known as the Kongma La (18,135 feet, 5527 m), Cho La (17,783 feet, 5420 m) and Renjo La (17,634 feet, 5375m). (Kongde, outlined above between Thame and Tok-Tok is sometimes referred to as the Fourth Pass).

A challenging circuit known as **The Three Passes** can be traversed under good weather conditions if you are acclimatized, fit and ambitiously looking for adventure. This course should be avoided if you have altitude symptoms and are not feeling physically fine. It traverses remote high elevation territory and the distances between facilities can be long and strenuous.

Of the four valleys, the route following the Khumbu Khola to Everest Base Camp is the most popular, the Dudh Kosi with Gokyo and dazzling lakes are second in popularity – both routes offer jaw-dropping, non-stop views! Chukhung might have the most well-endowed mountain scenery of all but sees less traffic, mostly because Everest is not visible in this valley due to the massive Lhotse-Nuptse headwall. The Bhote Kosi valley north of Thame is serene and has much to offer yet receives a relative trickle of tourists compared to the three other major valleys.

Most trekkers set their sights on Everest Base Camp, where mountaineering expeditions set up in April and May. It is the closest trekkers can get to the summit without being a climber although views of the pinnacle are not possible from base camp itself. Along this popular route from Namche to Everest Base Camp, you might even encounter strings of thirty or more trekkers in a group. Faster moving hikers might find themselves boxed in by slow groups. The bottlenecks and competition for limited rooms and facilities can be a bit of a surprise for people not used to crowds in the great outdoors. Tour groups are given priority at lodges over independent trekkers as groups usually spend more money and lodge owners are keen for their bookings and give privileges to guides who deliver repeat business. It makes smart business sense but can be frustrating to independent trekkers.

If you can be satisfied by breathtaking mountain scenery that does not include the closest possible proximity to Everest, then follow the alternative routes described within and leave the crowds of Everest Base Camp behind.

A reasonable itinerary for a 'Best of Khumbu' tour for those with at least three weeks would be to follow the 'Three Passes' in an anti-clockwise direction (facilities and acclimatization make an east to west traverse advisable). Each of these passes requires that you are acclimatized and physically fit and capable of negotiating difficult, sometimes exposed sections of trail.

The challenging Three Passes circuit itinerary is briefly outlined as follows:

-Namche to Tengoche en route to Chukhung. Explore the glorious upper reaches of the Imja Khola valley and be overpowered by thrilling views of some of the world's best mountain scenery – snowy gods and goddesses soaring skyward.

-Pass a sparkling emerald lake up to the first pass, the Kongma La, highest of the three passes and traverse across the Khumbu Khola valley to Lobuche.

-Head north up the Khumbu Khola valley to Gorek Shep, Kala Pattar viewpoint and Everest Base Camp.

-Return to Lobuche and head west over the second pass, Cho La, to traverse the Dudh Kosi valley to Gokyo

-Explore Gokyo and surrounding area including Gokyo Ri viewpoint and 'Scoundrel's Viewpoint' near the fifth lake.

-Ascend to the west of Gokyo, to traverse the third and final of the Three Passes circuit, the Renjo La. Descend by a beautiful alpine lake to the pristine Thame Valley and a centuries old trading route from Tibet to Thame. Thame village has the regal Thame Gomba perched above the hamlet and *The Thame Cultural Trail* to explore.

-Return to Namche with a side trail to the famous Lawudo Gomba along the way in an idyllic setting with an astonishing, sweeping panorama of the wide valley below. Alternatively, trek from Thame to Tok-Tok over the 'Fourth Pass' at Kongde.

Other options to consider for a 'best of' tour include exploring **Pangboche**, one of the Khumbu's oldest settlements and **Phortse**, another ancient settlement along the serene eastern route of the Dudh Kosi Valley to Gokyo.

NAMCHE BAZAAR TO EVEREST BASE CAMP (AND SIDE-TRIP TO CHUKHUNG) Chukhung is a highly recommended side-trip if you have a few extra days to spare. It departs from the Everest Base Camp Trek journey along the Imja Khola to the trekking outpost of Chukhung with a non-stop feast of mountain scenery. Both it and the journey to Everest Base Camp are outlined below starting from Namche Bazaar.

From **Namche Bazaar** the most direct trail to Tengboche rises to the saddle to the east, Chorgang (11,550 feet, 3520 m), where the Sagarmatha National Park headquarters and a museum are located. Meet the trail onward from a large boulder with eye-catching *mani* prayer inscriptions.

Contour high above the Dudh Kosi on a wide track with astonishing views of the Dudh Kosi Valley and revel at **the Himalayan goddesses dressed in white soaring ahead of you, including the presiding deity Chomolungma (Mt. Everest). Pass** *stupa* at dramatic ridgeline viewpoints. Along this section, you might encounter a man sitting trailside next to a large sign with translations in no less than four languages. He has been regularly soliciting donations for trail work to Everest Base Camp and has been doing it for years and years - - suspiciously too busy looking for donors than performing actual work. Of course, the decision to donate is up to you, and locals and officials condone it. If you feel

like giving, please donate only as much as locals do (otherwise, you might be reinforcing a common notion that foreigners have an over-abundance of money and too much to look after wisely).

Reach Kyangsuma, 1 hour from Chorgang and savor the splendid mountain panorama to the east with Thamserku, Ama Dablam, Kyangtema and Lhotse! Five minutes beyond is a trail junction and a sign pointing the way to Khumjung, Gokyo, and Tengboche and more lodges in **Sangnasa** (11,800 feet, 3597 m) within **1¼ hours** from Namche. Descend through a forested area, passing the quiet village of Trashinga with tea shops and lodging and more tea shops of Labisyasa in 20 minutes, and drop steeply to reach the Dudh Kosi at **Pungo Tenga** (10,650 feet, 3247 m) with a nearby bakery. Pungo Tenga has hotels on both banks of the Dudh Kosi, **1–1¼ hours** from Sangnasa **(2–2½ hours** from Namche Bazaar). After crossing the river, go through formalities at an army check post where your documents will be registered before a trudge up through rhododendron and juniper. There are rest stops along the way and impressive views of Kyangtema, a peak named for its shape as a saddle made of snow. Pass through a *kani* gateway (local belief is that the *kani* will cleanse impurities clinging to passersby and thereby keep the area and monastery safe from contaminations) near a large *stupa* of enchanting **Tengboche** (12,887 feet, 3867 m) some **1½-2 hours** from the river crossing at Pungo Tenga.

Ama Dablam rises vibrantly above it all, jutting into the heavens. She is perhaps the most elegant of all Himalayan peaks and nicknamed *The Matterhorn of the Himalaya*. Ama Dablam translates to *mother's jewel box* and the western aspect resembles a mother with arms reaching out with a hanging glacier as the *dablam*, a pendant commonly worn by Sherpa women. But she

can be a life taker. In 2010 a helicopter crashed killing both pilots on a rescue mission on its north face and an avalanche in 2006 took six climbers.

There is plentiful lodging at bustling Tengboche, although facilities might be at capacity during the high seasons (October to early November, and March-April). The area is administered by the monastery and has a porter shelter. A small hydropower station provides electricity and water is pumped up from Deboche. The monastery requests that you do not use a 'toilet tent' but instead patronize the recently constructed public toilets.

TENGBOCHE MONASTERY

Tengboche Monastery was founded in 1916 by Lama Gulu, and the monastery building was completed with the help of the local Sherpa community three years later. The main temple was destroyed in a 1934 earthquake and subsequently rebuilt. Electricity was established at the monastery in 1988, and in 1989 it was razed by fire from an electric heater accident. It was again rebuilt, this time with both foreign and local funding.

At the entrance is a foot imprint set in stone believed to be from Lama Sangwa Dorje who is credited with bringing Buddhism to the region in the 1700s. The monastery follows the Nyingma tradition, as do most Sherpa. If you visit the main hall during daily prayer and chanting ceremonies, you are in for an otherworldly experience. The sing-song rhythm of the chanting accompanied by bells, conch shell blasts, trumpets, drums, and cymbals leaves quite a lasting impression. Ceremonies usually take place in the early morning and early evening.

If you enter a monastery, do not sit on cushions or against pillars unless invited to do so, and obtain permission before taking photographs of the monks.

Tengboche's Visitor Center offers informative displays on Buddhism, Tibetan medicine and more as well as souvenirs for the trip home.

"An open, peaceful mind is very beneficial and helps others." – *Tengboche Rinpoche*

TIBETAN MEDICINE, THE ART OF HEALING

Sowa Rigpa translates to 'the art of healing', and is generally known *Sowa Rigpa* translates to 'the art of healing', and is more generally known as Tibetan medicine. This time-honored healing tradition dates back over two thousand years and shares ties and similarities with Indian ayurveda. *Sowa rigpa* and ayurveda are holistic and both aim to treat body and mind together. Focusing on the mind is considered most important.

According to *Sowa Rigpa* principles, **'Our state of mind and mood affects everything we do. When we are happy, our body is at ease and the world seems a brighter place. Even if we are sick we can be at peace. However, if we are sad our physical well-being goes unappreciated. Personal conduct and diet are considered two of the most important factors relating to health. Diet may be either conducive to curing disease or contribute to its cause...indiscriminate eating is like poisoning yourself.'**

The practice of *Sowa Rigpa* encompasses identification and harvest of rare Himalayan flora. Most of the medicinal plants (*jadibuti*) are collected from the highlands of Nepal and the Tibetan Plateau. The World Health Organization estimates that up to *'80% of the world's people depend on traditional medicine and plant extracts for their primary health care needs.'*

Amchi (healers) prepare their own compounds, diagnose patients, and prescribe remedies as needed. A consultation with an a*mchi* generally includes manual measuring of wrist pulse strength and speed, checking the coloring of the tongue and whites of the eyes and more. Herbal remedies are usually handcrafted at an in-house dispensary.

Amchi are typically skilled in astrology, too, analyzing the stars and forecasting favorable and unfavorable dates. They are consulted for general readings and specific timings and compatibility of travel plans, activities, events (e.g., wedding dates) and more based on stellar alignments and lunar phases among other aspects of a client's horoscope.

Sowa Rigpa is a classic art true to its ancient roots and has not been altered by the modern, turbulent world but can help cure its ills.

TENGBOCHE TO TSURO WOG

From **Tengboche** the trail heads east and descends slightly, past lodges some 15-20 minutes beyond and 400 feet (122 m) lower at **Deboche** where there is a nearby nunnery (Ani Gomba).

Continue past more lodging at Milinggo in 15 more minutes, all the while traveling in a charming moss-festooned forest above the river. Continue to the Imja Khola, and cross on a steel bridge (12,400 feet, 3780 m), from which you have a dazzling view of Ama Dablam towering to the east. Pass a *stupa* and beyond a *kani* gateway and the trail diverges. The left (higher) trail ascends to Pangboche Gomba (13,075 feet, 3985 m) at the settlement of Upper Pangboche, while the more direct trail to the right leads to Lower **Pangboche** (12,800 feet, 3901 m), some **1¼ hours** from Tengboche. There are plentiful lodges to choose from in both areas, and the lower area, because it is along the direct route, is much more popular with tourists.

Pangboche Gomba is the oldest in Khumbu, built around 300 years ago when Buddhism was introduced to the Khumbu by Lama Sangwa Dorje. According to legend, Lama Sangwa Dorje cast a handful of hair near the *gomba;* a grove of juniper trees sprouted from the hair and the grove is considered the dwelling place of local spirits. Because of the spirits and association with the *gomba,* these trees are sacred and have been saved from use as firewood. Upper Pangboche is a calmer and quieter place to stay relative to the crowds of Lower Pangboche.

Continue northeast to reach the junction above a cantilever bridge over the Imja Khola (which is not crossed). You are rising above tree line. The trail might be icy between Pangboche and Shomare (13,287 feet, 4050m), reached in 45 minutes. Shomare is a pleasant place to overnight with comfortable lodges that are often overlooked and therefore, the location is much less busy than Pangboche.

The landscape becomes more arid and barren as you arrive at lodging of Orsho within 15 minutes. In 15 more minutes, or **1¼–1½hours** beyond Pangboche, the trail divides above **Tsuro Wog (aka, Warsa)**, a small summer herding pasture with seasonal stone dwellings (13,725 ft, 4183 m).

Dingboche or Pheriche?

The right branch just beyond Tsuro Wog goes to Dingboche, while the left fork leads to Pheriche; both destinations can be reached in the same time, and from both one can continue to

Kala Pattar and Everest Base Camp.

Both Dingboche and Pheriche have plentiful lodges to choose from; phone service is available, as well as Internet, and batteries can be charged. Dingboche is more popular with tourists and therefore Pheriche might be preferable for trekkers looking for a more relaxed atmosphere. It offers a great place to bask in the surrounding beauty of the snowy titans peering down at you.

It is advised to spend time at Pheriche or Dingboche for adequate acclimatization. On a 'rest day', depending on where you have stopped, visit Pheriche/Dingboche and farther east up the Imja Khola, as described later, or climb a ridge to the north/northeast to as high as 17,000 ft/5180 m (and even higher to Nagatsang Peak at 18,208 ft/5550 m for magnificent views of Makalu (world's 5th highest peak) to the east and other vibrant summits. You could also cross the Khumbu Khola and climb up on the shoulders of Taboche to the west, or simply do the next day's walk without your full pack and return to Pheriche/Dingboche for the night. If you are feeling the effects of altitude, then visit the Pheriche HRA aid-post. All visitors would be wise to attend the lecture on altitude illness, usually given at 3 PM daily during the busy seasons (October to early November, and March-April).

Tsuro Wog (aka, Warsa) to Dingboche

At the trail junction 15 minutes beyond the lodge at Orsho, and 1¼–1½ hours from Pangboche, take the right-hand branch. Descend to a bridge just above the confluence of the Khumbu and Imja rivers, and cross the Khumbu (also known as Lobuche) Khola. Continue heading east along the true right side of the Imja Khola into the Imja valley, climbing gently to Dingboche (14,304 feet, 4360 m), ¾-1 hour or about 2–3 hours from Pangboche, depending on your pace and capability.

Tsuro Wog (aka, Warsa) to Dingboche via Pheriche

From the trail junction 15 minutes beyond the lodge at Orsho, 1¼–1½ hours from Pangboche, the trail to Pheriche climbs to the crest of a small ridge (14,050 feet, 4282 m) marked by a cairn (local tradition is to pick up a nearby rock and drop it onto the pile as you pass by). Descend a short distance to the bridge over the Khumbu (aka, Lobuche) Khola (13,875 feet, 4229 m) and cross it to the west (left) bank to reach Pheriche (13,950 feet, 4252 m) in 35–40 minutes, some 2–3 hours from Pangboche, depending on acclimatization.

Pheriche has a Trekker's Aid Post set up by the Himalayan Rescue Association in 1973 and staffed by volunteer physicians during the tourist season to provide medical care to trekkers and porters. There are also daily lectures during the peak seasons regarding acclimatization safety at 3 pm; these lectures are frequently given in Dingboche, too. Consultations at the clinic can be arranged for the equivalent of $50 USD (more if after hours and more for 'house calls'), credit cards accepted at 5% extra fee. The consultation fee for Nepalis is 50 NRS.

To continue on to Dingboche, climb up and over the ridge (14,250 feet, 4343 m) behind HRA's trekker's aid post at Pheriche and descend to **Dingboche** in **35–45 minutes**.

DINGBOCHE TO CHUKHUNG AND THE IMJA KHOLA VALLEY

Imja Khola Valley is enveloped by snowy peaks and non-stop mountain views. This side trip is perhaps even more spectacular than the popular areas of the Khumbu, however, views of Everest are missing. Merely for that reason, the area is less visited and much less crowded. That said, Lhotse (ranking as the world's 4th highest), dominates to the north

and Makalu (5th highest) can be seen from selected viewpoints. The other surrounding snow-covered goddesses are beautiful beyond compare. This side route is recommended for those who have the time or in exchange for more crowded trails of the Khumbu.

From Dingboche, the trail follows the Imja Khola and passes below the seasonal herder village (no facilities) of Bibre in 1 hour from Dingboche.

The trail to Chukhung continues toward the east, passing a teashop (and plans for a lodge) at **Dusum** in **1½ hours** from Dingoche. Continue on with unrelenting views, the Lhotse-Nuptse wall competes to steal the show. Imja Tse (Island Peak, 20,253 feet, 6173 m), Nepal's most popular climbing peak, stands alone among a sea of giants and a new perspective of Ama Dablam (her north face) will bedazzle.

Cross numerous streams that flow from the Nuptse and Lhotse Glaciers, to **Chukhung** (15,535 feet, 4734 m) in **30 minutes** from Dusum. Chukhung is the uppermost settlement of this valley and has many lodges and shops that rent mountaineering gear, mostly for climbers aiming for Island Peak, Nepal's most popular climbing destination.

Chukhung Ri (18,238 feet, 5559 m), to the north of Chukhung, is inexplicably considered a 'Group A Trekking Peak' and as such it technically requires special fees to reach its summit (which involves a challenging rock scramble). Perhaps it will be reclassified, but there have been no reports of officials checking for permits, and many foreigners visit the peak without permits. Alternatively, you can ascend a slightly lesser crest. Both the peak itself and the lesser summit provide whopping viewpoints of the high elevation amphitheater you are in as well as of the west face of Makalu. Another option is Chukhung Tse peak (19,160 feet, 5840 m), northwest of Chukhung Ri, but a direct route is hazardous. This peak is best attempted by heading up the draw northeast from Chukhung and then approaching it from the east, a full day's journey, out and back.

Enjoy the astonishingly vibrant views of Lhotse and Nuptse. Imja Tse (Island Peak) is to the east of Chukhung and received over 6000 climbers in 2012 and requires a certified guide, extra fees and technical equipment. A popular day trip is out and back to Island Peak Base Camp south of the peak itself (2-2½ hours each way). Near base camp is Imja Tsho lake with unrelenting views of the skyscraping mountains (including Baruntse, Lhotse, Nuptse, the northeast face of Ama Dablam and more) and nearby glaciers, including Imja Glacier.

CLIMATE CHANGE VERSUS THE MIGHTY HIMALAYA

There are some 3000 glaciers and 1500 glacial lakes in Nepal above 11,500 ft (3500 m). It is predicted that a 4°C rise in the global average temperature, which is within some projections for the end of this century, would eliminate these glaciers. According to Nepal's Department of Hydrology and Meteorology (DHM), the temperature in Nepal's Himalaya may be increasing by an average of 0.04° Celsius per year.

Imja Glacier is considered to be one of the fastest-retreating Himalayan glaciers at approximately 243 feet (74 m) per year, and the decline is attributed to solar warming. Imja Tsho Lake has increased in size alarmingly over the last half century from mere melt ponds in the 1950s to a lake of nearly 0.38 square mile (1 km²), or 247.11 acres, with an estimated volume of 47 million cubic yards (35 million m³) of water and rising. Its moraine of rock and ice is considered unstable and a threat for a glacial lake outburst flood (GLOF).

If extensive, a GLOF could result in severe wreckage downstream. A 2002 report by the International Centre for Integrated Mountain Development (ICIMOD) and the UN Environment Program puts twenty of Nepal's glacial lakes at risk for a GLOF, and Imja Tsho is considered the worst danger. According to Nepal's Department of Hydrology and Meteorology, there have been more than fourteen GLOFs in Nepal. The most recent in the Khumbu was recorded in September 1998, which caused flooding on the Inkhu Khola. Other floods in the Khumbu include ones that damaged parts of Ghat in 1985 and Pangboche in 1979. In May 2012, a massive landslide near Machhapuchhre in the Annapurna Region caused flooding on the Seti River and dozens of people perished. In early August, 2014 a tragic landslide in Sindhupalchowk District (west of Solu-Khumbu along the Arniko Highway to Tibet) killed over 150 people.

"Climbing is becoming more and more dangerous because glaciers and snow are melting and rock is appearing and avalanches are more frequent. The impact of global warming is visible in the high Himalaya," Ang Tshering Sherpa, President, Nepal Mountaineering Association.

CHUKUNG TO LOBUCHE BY WAY OF THE KONGMA LA.

A high route from Chukhung to Lobuche crosses the challenging high pass to the northwest known as the Kongma La (18,135 feet, 5527 m) (The first of the Three Passes Circuit). There are no facilities along this route until Lobuche, a long, strenuous day that traverses loose shale, boulders and a wide, glaciated valley. Pokalde Peak (19,048 feet, 5806m), south of the pass, might be climbed for those with extra time, ambition, energy and skill, but it is technically a regulated peak and requires permits. Head west from the lower lodges of Chukung and cross a nearby stream. Find the trail that ascends to the west along the foothills.

The pass is some 4 hours from Chukhung and nearby its base are several alpine lakes, the largest is a mesmerizing emerald green. Take in the majestic views before descending into the Khumbu valley to the northwest and passing through a boulder field before reaching the valley floor. Climb the eastern lateral moraine of the Khumbu glacier. Work your way west across the desolate glacier following previous trails that you can find to reach Lobuche on the western side, some 2½ hours from the pass (see below for Lobuche onward to Everest Base Camp).

DINGBOCHE TO THUKLA

If continuing toward Everest from **Dingboche**, ascend to the ridge above the lodges to follow a tranquil high route above the Khumbu River valley. You will have enviable views of the natural setting including the peaks of Ama Dablam, Thamserku, Cholatse, Taboche, Lobuche, and even a glimpse of Pumo-Ri. Continue through scenic pasturing area and seasonal dwellings and meet the direct trail from Pheriche where the route descends to cross a glacial stream for a brief uphill to Thukla in **1½–2¼ hours** from Dingboche.

PHERICHE TO THUKLA

If heading on from **Pheriche** to the foot of Everest, continue north along the flats of the valley floor for 30-40 minutes to Phulang Kala, a settlement of stone dwellings populated during the pasture season of the monsoon (June-September). Follow the grassy lateral moraine of the Khumbu Glacier. The route meets the upper trail from Dingboche before descending to cross a glacial stream and a brief uphill to the lodges at **Thukla** (15,075 feet, 4593 m), 1-1¼ hours from Phulang Kala (**1½–2 hours** from Pheriche). (If headed west to the Cho La pass, rather than north to Lobuche and Everest Base Camp, then please follow the description below **Thukla to Cho La**).

THUKLA TO KALA PATTAR AND EVEREST BASE CAMP

If you have a headache or other symptoms that altitude might be affecting you, then rest at Thukla until the symptoms improve or descend lower if they worsen. Do not continue upward and risk greater complications.

Accommodations at Thukla and above may be limited in peak season (autumn and spring) and early starts are advised to reach the next accommodations before the crowds. Proceed by climbing steeply to a crest (15,879 feet, 4840 m) with stone memorials built for climbers who have perished on expeditions to the many summits of this region. Views here are marvelous and the crest is a fine place for a break. Contour on the west side of the glacier. After crossing another stream of melt water, the trail heads northeast, gradually rising to many facilities including a few strikingly massive lodges at **Lobuche** (16,175 feet, 4930 m), situated below the terminal moraine of Lobuche Glacier. Lobuche is **1½-2 hours** from Thukla and a climb to the ridge crest to the west is rewarded with wondrous views, especially at sunset when Mother Nature lights up the peaks in shades of burnt orange, peach and red.

A PYRAMID IN THE KHUMBU
Just north of Lobuche is The Pyramid International Laboratory-Observatory, an Italian-built compound that includes an intriguing pyramid structure made of glass. Researchers generally arrive in spring and autumn to conduct projects in glaciology and sedimentology in the surrounding areas, as well as physiology and medicine. This research center has a meteorological station that collects data on monsoon development and other phenomena such as pollution levels, and houses a seismological station as well. Additionally, the lab is fitted with a GPS to measure long-term tectonic movements together with other regional GPS stations. Raw data from the laboratory and more information can be found at http://evk2.isac.cnr.it and www.evk2cnr.org/cms/en (and, if you are fluent in Italian, visit http://www2.units.it/telegeom).

It is the very collision of subcontinental plates (the Indo-Australian and Eurasian) that led to the uprising of the world's highest range and Nepal's greatest natural attraction, the Himalaya. The event is still occurring and the Himalaya are said to be growing several millimeters each year with India drifting toward the northeast Tibetan Frontier at around 18 mm (0.7 in) per year.

The laboratory also has rescue equipment that might be of assistance in an emergency. The trail turnoff to the pyramid laboratory is **15-20 minutes** north of Lobuche (to the left from the trail to Gorak Shep) and then less than 10 minutes up the trail from the main route.

LOBUCHE AND BEYOND
It is possible to use Lobuche as a base to climb to Kala Pattar for wondrous views and then return in the same, long day. This is advisable to lessen altitude sickness issues at the higher overnight location of Gorak Shep.

Beyond **Lobuche** the trail contours a trough beside the Khumbu Glacier before climbing up the side of Changri Glacier's lateral moraine and then passing through it. **Gorak Shep** (17,008 feet, 5184 m) is reached in **2-3 hours** from Lobuche. This otherworldly location has a collection of some of the highest lodges in the world which will be crowded during the trekking season. Do not expect too many frills here, especially given the altitude and remoteness, although comforts are continually being added and even internet might be available and relatively expensive. The lodges' cozy dining rooms are usually the warmest places to hang out. You will have a chance to meet a motley crew of fellow adventure travelers from around the world, here to savor the surrounding mountainous Nirvana just like you.

The triangular face of Nuptse soars majestically above Gorak Shep to the west. The porter shelter in the area was built through the efforts of Community Action Nepal (CAN) and the International Porter Protection Group (IPPG).

There are usually a few Tibetan snow cocks in this area. They travel together and have the appearance of a portly partridge or chukkar, and can often be approached quite closely.

Gorak Shep is the starting point for one of the world's highest marathon races, the Everest Marathon to Namche Bazaar (including a journey to Thame and back), which began in 1987 as a charitable-event (www.everestmarathon.org.uk). Another marathon, the annual Tenzing Norgay Marathon, was begun in 2003 and is held on May 29th to commemorate the first ascent of Everest (www.everestmarathon.com). It

begins at Everest Base Camp and finishes at Namche Bazaar. (See also ww.trailrunningnepal.org for other running opportunities in Nepal.)

Kala Pattar The popular viewpoint of **Kala Pattar** (Sanskrit for 'Black Rock') is at 18,208 feet/ 5550 m and can be reached in **1½ hours** from Gorak Shep. A banquet of peaks awaits you there. View Everest and her sister peaks, standing out radiantly with the Khumbu Glacial Valley below floating away from these goddesses.

The Nepalese government held a cabinet meeting on Kala Pattar's nearby plateau on December 4, 2009, a week ahead of that year's world summit on climate change in Copenhagen. Their goal was to draw attention to ramifications in the Himalaya of increased weather imbalances due to modifications in climate.

Many people make an early start to arrive at Kala Pattar by sunrise, and the weather is generally clearer in the mornings in the Himalaya. However, the position of the sun in relation to the peaks makes the viewpoint more favorable later rather than earlier. Dusk provides unforgettable views of a skyline drenched in color with peaks jutting into the heavens and dancing in different hues. Staying for the sunset feast

61

makes for a long, eerie descent at twilight. *If you hike up for the evening show, bring a flashlight for the long return back and then enjoy your memories over a well-deserved hot meal and night of rest back at the lodge.* As you return by flashlight to the lodges, all the while encircled by silent, spectral titans covered in snow and ice you might feel like you are on a distant, icy planet. The wind moans over the barren landscape, and on clear nights, stars twinkle brightly above it all.

JOURNEY TO BASE CAMP

The site of **base camp** that is used for climbing the south side of **Everest** is near to the foot of the astonishing Khumbu Icefall (17,575 feet, 5357 m) and can be reached from **Gorak Shep** in 1¾–2¾ hours. **Mountain climbing season is typically April and May when the jet stream hits the summit with less force and temperatures are milder. It generally takes climbers forty or so days to reach the top allowing for acclimatization to altitude and rest days.**

To head to base camp, begin from the flat, sandy area to the northeast of Gorak Shep; pass memorials and work through boulders to follow the lateral moraine before venturing over the rubble-covered surface of the Khumbu Glacier. There are no views of Everest's summit from the base camp area, although you will be surrounded by peaks soaring skyward and Everest can be seen en route.

There is no accommodation for trekkers at base camp, although during the season enterprising Sherpa might be selling food items and drinks there.

In 2003, Luanne Freer, M.D., set up an emergency outpost clinic for the climbing season of April and May for anyone who needs it. See www.everestER.org for more information. This clinic is associated with HRA's Pheriche medical station.

Physicians in the high-altitude Khumbu region have noted that the three most common ailments are the following:

> **-bronchitis, aka, 'Khumbu cough,' brought on by cold, arid conditions**
>
> **-gastroenteritis**
>
> **-viral upper-respiratory infections**.

It is possible to visit the base camp from Lobuche and return in the same long day if you are well acclimatized. You can vary your return trip from Gorak Shep by heading back down the valley to Pheriche and Pangboche or climbing over the Cho La, the high pass linking to the Gokyo valley to the west.

CHOMOLUNGMA - EVEREST – SAGARMATHA

The world's highest mountain is named after Sir George Everest (pronounced 'Eve-rest'), Surveyor General of the Survey of India from 1823 to 1843. The Trigonometric Survey of India Team officially announced Mt. Everest as the planet's highest peak in 1856. At the time, the peak was called Peak XV. In 1865, it was re-named in honor of Sir Everest. Sherpas use its Tibetan name, Chomolungma, where resides one of five sister deities of long life, Chomolungma (aka, *Chomo Miyo Lang Sangma*, the sister that provides sustenance).

The Nepali name, *Sagarmatha*, translates to the top of the planet reaching the ocean of the heavens (a liberal interpretation of the Sanskrit). Current estimates of its height above sea level are 29,022.6 feet (8846.1 m), plus 8.4 feet (2.55 m) of snow and ice, making it 29,031 feet (8848.65 m) high! The summit is generally listed at 8848 m and that is with about 3.5 m of snow, thus the top, not counting the snow, is at nearly 8844.5 m.

A Brief History of Everest Climbing

-Although George Everest was head of the Survey of India from 1823 to 1843, he neither set foot near nor even saw the peak that honors his name.

-The mountain was first explored by outsiders from the Tibetan side in 1921 after gaining permission to access it from the Dalai Lama. The early climbing expeditions were on the Tibet side before climbing efforts were interrupted by WWII. Following the war, a joint British U.S. group visited the south side in 1950, and climbing attention shifted to Nepal.

-The mountain was first climbed in 1953 by Edmund Percival Hillary and Tenzing Norgay Sherpa. Two days prior to the monumental feat, a pair of British climbers from the same team approached within 90 m/300 feet of the summit but turned back for lack of oxygen supply. Hillary acknowledged that if the earlier duo had not broken trail and cached supplies, then he and Norgay likely would not have made the summit themselves.

-The Swiss reached the summit the following year, and the mountain rested undisturbed until 1963, when a US team climbed it by the West Ridge and came down the original route, the first traverse of the mountain.

-1965, Nawang Gombu Sherpa became the first to summit twice (first in 1963 with a US expedition and in 1965 with an Indian expedition)

-Junko Tabei of Japan became the first female summiteer in 1975.

-1978 Reinhold Messner and Peter Haebeler summited without oxygen

-1980 Yasuo Kato of Japan was the first non-Sherpa to reach the summit more than once (1973 was his first ascent).

-1980 Messner summited solo and without oxygen

-1980 A Polish team achieved the first winter ascent (also first winter ascent of any of the fourteen 8,000-plus meter peaks.

-1988 Jean-Marc Boivin paraglided from the summit to Camp 2.

-By 1990 Everest was being exploited by commercial expeditions that tantalized inexperienced mountaineers into paying large sums. Recent carnage reminds us of the powerful forces that effect the human theater on the world's highest terrain.

-1993, Pasang Lhamu Sherpa became the first Nepali female to summit Everest. She perished on the descent and posthumously has become a Nepali national heroine. A peak has been named in her honor as well as a statue in Kathmandu near Baudhnath. Additionally, in Lukla, a *kani* (gateway) heading north out of town as well as the memorial hospital at the southern end both are graced with her name.

-1999, Babu Chiri Sherpa spent 21 hours on the summit without supplementary oxygen. (He also was a record holder for fastest ascent at just under 17 hours. He died on the mountain in 2001 during his 11th attempt at the summit)

-2000, Davo Karničar descended from the summit on skis.

-2001, Marco Siffredi snowboarded from the summit

-2002, Erk Weihenmayer was the first blind summiteer

-2004, Pemba Dorje Sherpa made the fastest ascent (along the southern approach and with supplemental oxygen), in 8 hours and 10 minutes

-2005, Didier Delsalle landed a helicopter on the summit (not without controversy) setting records for both highest landing and takeoff.

-2008, Nepal's Min Bahadur Sherchan became Nepal's oldest summiteer at 76 (25 days shy of age 77)

-2012, Japan' Tamae Watanabe, 73 years old became the oldest woman to climb Everest

-2010 13 year old Jordan Romero is the youngest summiteer (not without controversy at putting a young person in risky circumstances).

China has since implemented rules banning people under 18 from attempting Everest and Nepal sets the bar at 16.

-Nepal's Phurba Tashi Sherpa and Apa Sherpa have both summited 21 times! Phurba Tashi has summited 8,000 m peaks a record 30 times, including 21 of Everest, (in 2007 he summited 3 times, twice in 2011). Apa Sherpa has summited an average of once a year for over twenty years (however, he summited twice in 1992 (but did not summit in 1996 and 2001). The record for a non-Sherpa is 14 times by Dave Hahn of the USA.

-23rd May, 2010, 169 climbers reached the summit, the most ever on a single day!

-May, 2012 Sano Babu Sunwar and Lakpa Sherpa tandem paraglided from the summit. They landed near Syangboche and continued their journey by foot and then by kayak to the Bay of Bengal near Kolkata, India. Their astonishing *Summit to Sea* effort earned them National Geographic Adventurers of the Year, 2012!

-May 23rd, 2013, Yuichiro Miura became the oldest summiteer at 80 years old! He also holds the distinction of being the first person to ski on Everest which he did from the South Col in 1970. *The Man Who Skied Down Everest* was a film about the feat that won the Academy Award for Best Documentary!

-April 18th, 2014, Sixteen Nepali climbers perished (mostly Sherpa) in an avalanche between Camp I and Camp II.

-Sometimes referred to as an 'Icy Graveyard,' in the history of climbing on the peak to 2013, around 250 climbers have died including nearly 90 Sherpa. A majority of the corpses are still on the mountain!

-An extensive, valuable database of information on climbing in Everest and Nepal and its border peaks is available primarily because of a longtime chronicler of Everest expeditions, Elizabeth Hawley, who began archiving data in 1963. For more information on Everest, including climbing statistics, visit www.everestnews.com, and www.himalayandatabase.com.

LOBUCHE TO GOKYO OVER THE CHO LA HIGH PASS

Trekkers feeling fit and fine can consider crossing Cho La, a challenging high pass offering access from the Khumbu River Valley of Everest to the Dudh Kosi River Valley of Gokyo. The traverse requires bouldering at times but offers sensational up close views of Cholatse (20,784 feet, 6335 m), Taboche (20,889 feet, 6367 m) and the Lobuche massif. It involves a short glacier crossing, and most people cross without a rope and ice axe; however, these items of gear provide added safety. After a fresh snowfall, avoid this journey until new tracks are made by experienced guides. Lodging facilities are available at Dzonglha (Everest side) and Thangnak (Gokyo side).

LOBUCHE TO DZONGLHA

Begin by retracing your steps south from **Lobuche** following a stream. Continue for 20 minutes along the lateral moraine as far as the stream crossing. Instead of crossing (which then descends to Thukla), the trail to Dzonglha and the Cho La pass branches to the right to continue along the west side of the valley. Eventually, the route reaches a ridge and turns northwest into the valley of the pass to contour high above the magnificent Chola Tsho lake. Cross through a depression in the valley before ascending to **Dzonglha** (15,869 feet, 4843 m) in **2½–3 hours** from Lobuche. The inns are surrounded by majestic crags soaring into the sky that seem but a stone's throw away. Lodging might be packed with tourists on the way up to or coming down from the pass, but the awe-inspiring scenery can be overpowering and Dzonglha is an enchanting place to spend the night.

THUKLA TO DZONGLHA AND THE CHO LA

If you happen to be coming from **Thukla** along the main EBC route, then the trail to Dzonglha and the Cho La heads west from Thukla to cross a stream and then splits. The right branch ascends steeply to meet the trail coming from Lobuche to Dzonglha. Stay left to contour more evenly to reach Chola Tsho lake in **30 minutes** and enjoy the breathtaking views of turquoise waters below majestic crags soaring into the sky. The trail follows the north shore of the lake and rises gradually to meet the upper trail near Chola Og (15,305 feet, 4665 m), a pasture area with seasonal huts, in **1¼-1½ hours**. **Dzonglha** (15,889 feet, 4843 m) with three inns, is another **15-20 minutes** up the trail.

DZONGLHA TO THANGNAK TRAVERSING THE CHO LA

Cross over a small crest from Dzonglha and descend slightly into a wide valley. Cross streams to work your way up to the head of the valley. Climb through loose rock and then steeply up through and over boulders. Look for cairns and painted green arrows to indicate the ascent route. Eventually, gain the glacier just before the pass and keep to its south side on the snow-covered surface. For safety, try to follow whatever path has been previously made. The surface might be bare ice and thus slippery and crampons can be useful. Porters sometimes make do with cord lashed around the soles of their footwear for traction. Be aware that crevasses may be covered by snow and also may be near the *bergschrund* where the glacier pulls away from the rock. The pass (17,783 feet, 5420 m), is marked by cairns strung with prayer flags at least **2½–3 hours** from Dzonglha. New vistas open up before you, and the rugged trail that goes on to Thangnak can be made out below.

The descent from the pass is hazardously steep, sometimes over hard snow and rock. Be aware of loose stones and rock fall. Eventually you pass through scree to reach the valley floor and a boulder field and continue through it to a saddle to the west. Look for cairns to mark the way. Cross minor ridges, and descend steeply to reach **Thangnak** (15,387 feet, 4690 m), with seven substantial lodges and a few stone-built dwellings. It takes **2½-3 hours** from the pass to

Thangnak in good conditions (**4½-6 hours** or more from Dzonglha).

To continue to Gokyo, proceed up the lateral moraine to a cairned notch, and then make a surreal traverse of Nepal's largest glacier, the Ngozumpa Glacier. This wild path changes with the seasons as more and more melt-water begins to intersect and redirect the route. Ascend the moraine's western wall and come out to join the sublime setting of Gokyo along the shores of the enchanting third lake, less than **2 hours** from Thangnak. (See the section below about Gokyo for a description of this tantalizing area.)

GORAK SHEP TO PANGBOCHE AND PHORTSE

An excellent variation on the route back, for those not crossing the Cho La is to retrace your steps and head to Upper Pangboche. From there, traverse the trail over to Phortse, then either head up to Gokyo, or cross the Dudh Kosi and climb up to Khumjung and Namche. This thrilling, high traverse, sometimes with precipitous drop-offs, from **Pangboche** to **Phortse** takes **2–3 hours**. There is a good chance en route to see Himalayan tahr and other wildlife in their natural habitat as well as around the villages.

Phortse (12,500 feet, 3810m) is a traditional Sherpa village that lies on a plateau between the routes up the valleys to Everest Base Camp and Gokyo lakes. Silver birch and rhododendron thickets surround the settlement. Phortse has its own hydropower station and several lodges with some eighty households. Quite a few of the home-grown residents have scaled Everest on mountaineering expeditions.

PHORTSE TO GOKYO

From Phortse you can follow an isolated, serene trail that stays above and to the east of the Dudh Kosi to reach Na and continue on to Gokyo. This route is described below in reverse in the section on return options from Gokyo. Still another option is to bypass Na

and continue on the secluded east side of the valley to connect with Thangnak before continuing to Gokyo by crossing the Ngozumpa Glacier.

Alternatively, the other side of the valley has more facilities and foot traffic. To travel up to Gokyo on the main trail, then descend from Phortse to cross the Dudh Kosi in 30 minutes to Phortse Tenga. There you reach the usual route from Namche to Gokyo that heads along the west side of the Dudh Kosi to ascend to Dole in 1½-2 hours from the bridge. If going to back to Namche, then head south after crossing the bridge. (See the next section below for more detailed information on these routes.).

NAMCHE BAZAAR TO GOKYO

The Dudh Kosi (Milk River) Valley has jaw-dropping mountain vistas and a natural landscape replete with sparkling alpine lakes at the foot of the snow-topped peaks. The astonishing, non-stop views along the way offer a suitable alternative to the trek to Everest Base Camp -- all of the magnificence of the Himalaya and less of the crowds. Gokyo Ri viewpoint rivals Kala Pattar with an extensive panorama revealing four 8,000 m peaks and the twinkling turquoise lake below alongside Nepal's largest glacier, all vying for attention. Lodging is available along this route up to this third lake. However, from Namche, the direct route to Gokyo rapidly gains elevation, and if you are not already acclimatized then it will be necessarily to keep your days short and ascend at a safe pace while watching for signs of altitude sickness. If doing both the Everest Base Camp trail and this route, then it is advised to visit Gokyo after Everest Base Camp for better acclimatization. There are at least five choices to reach Gokyo in the Dudh Kosi Valley.

-The direct route from Namche passes through Kyangsuma to the trail junction near Sangnasa and north to Gokyo up the Dudh Kosi Valley.

-Alternatively, spend a night in Kunde or Khumjung (described above) to assist the acclimatization process. The trail departs from the eastern edge of Khumjung and meets up with the trail from Namche just north of Sangnasa to travel on to Gokyo along the west side of the Dudh Kosi Valley.

-Another option to Gokyo is by way of charming Phortse, perhaps reached from upper Pangboche on a return from Everest Base Camp. The trail from Phortse travels up the remote east side of the Dudh Kosi Valley, with few facilities en route (described below in reverse).

-Alternatively, after visiting Kala Pattar and Everest Base Camp, cross the challenging high pass, Cho La to reach Thangnak and then Gokyo after traversing the Ngozumpa Glacier.

-Finally, you could head north from Thame up the remote Bhote Kosi valley and over the Renjo La. Most people cross this high pass in the other direction for a better acclimatization regimen.

NAMCHE BAZAAR TO GOKYO, MONG DANDA VIA KYANGSUMA

This route follows the main trail up the west side of the Gokyo valley. Climb from **Namche Bazaar** to the saddle to the east, Chorgang (where the Sagarmatha National Park headquarters and a private museum are located). Catch the trail onward from a boulder with elegant *mani* inscriptions and contour high above the Dudh Kosi valley on a wide track, past lodges of **Kyangsuma, an hour from Chorgang. Five minutes beyond is a trail junction**, just before reaching **Sangnasa**. From here a trail ascends to join the direct trail from Khumjung in ten minutes and continues to **Mong Danda** (13,000 feet, 3962 m), the entrance to the Gokyo valley in **another hour, 2¼ hours** from Namche.

Namche to Mong Danda via Khumjung

This option from Namche climbs to the airfield of Syangboche. Beyond the airstrip the trail divides; head right for Khumjung and on to Mong Danda. Or, more favorably, spend a night in **Kunde or Khumjung** (mentioned above as day-hike options from Namche) for better acclimatization.

The trail to Mong Danda heads left at the east end of Khumjung and contours along the southeastern side of the sacred

Khumbi-Yul-Lha mountain. A steep trail to the left is to be avoided. Stay to the right, and a little farther along, the trail from Sangnasa ties in. Ascend stone steps and after crossing a prominence, stay left at another fork. Reach **Mong Danda,** at a crest of a ridge (13,000 feet, 3962 m), with a *stupa,* lodges, and a thrilling panoramic view of the valley and robust peaks soaring above it, **1¼-1½ hours** from Khumjung.

Mong Danda to Maccherma

The trail descends steeply to **Phortse Tenga** (11,950 feet, 3643 m) with lodges in **45 minutes** and diverges at the first lodge. The right branch descends to lodges near the riverside in ten minutes and continues to a bridge across the river followed by a climb to Phortse. Keep left fot the direct track to Dole and Gokyo. Pass an abandoned national park office and old army post, originally built to check poaching, but no longer in use. Cross several tributaries on wooden or iron bridges (with nearby waterfalls) and climb through timberland to **Dole** (13,400 feet, 4084 m), a pleasant locale with a babbling brook and many lodges, a **1½-2 hours** hike from Phortse Tenga.

The trail contours above the meadow of Gyele with seasonal stone-built dwellings, to Lafarma (14,200 feet, 4328 m), with a charming lodge in **45 minutes**. It continues to **Luza** (14,304 feet, 4360 m), in a small tributary valley, with more inns. In the next tributary valley is **Machherma** (14,485 feet, 4415 m), with many lodges, reached in **1-1¼ hours** from Lafarma, 2 hours from Dole. Similar to the HRA rescue post in Pheriche, the Machherma rescue post (at the western end of the settlement) offers lectures during the high seasons (October to early November, and March-April) and provides information on acclimatization, altitude sickness, and porter safety. The clinic and porter shelter was set up and is run by the International Porters Protection Group (IPPG) with assistance from Community Action Nepal (CAN), and is staffed by international volunteers (potential donors can find them online, www.charitygiving.co.uk, Reg #1143221). The post has a portable altitude chamber, two oxygen concentrators, a stretcher, medication, and more. Consultations can be arranged for the equivalent of $50 USD, 20 NRS for locals and trek agency staff and no-charge for porters.

From Machherma, continue **40 minutes** to **Pangka** (14,633 feet, 4460 m), with lodging. A powerful snowstorm in November 1995 dumped over 6.5 feet (2 m) of snow and caused an avalanche here that killed trekkers and porters in a lodge that was nestled against the hillside. The lodges here no longer abut the hillside.

A trail drops down from Phangka to Na at a crossing to the east side of the valley, providing a return option to Phortse and Namche, described below.

From Pangka, descend slightly, following a glacial melt river that flows down the west side of the Ngozumpa Glacier. The trail climbs steeply to the side of the lateral moraine and follows an outlet stream from the Gokyo lakes. Cross the stream on a bridge and arrive at the first small, shallow lake (15,450 ft/4709 m) in ¾-1 hour.

The trail is more level now and the second lake (15,511 ft/4728 m) is reached in 15-20 more minutes. Continue to the breathtaking scenery of the third lake (sometimes called Dudh Pokhari) in another 30 minutes, less than 2 hours from Pangka. The large, third lake is nestled at the foot of soaring peaks with many cozy tourist lodges and even an art gallery (it bills itself as the world's highest art gallery). The collection of lodges lie on the northeast shores of the glimmering turquoise lake and collectively are known as Gokyo (15,666 feet/4775 m). An outpost of the Machherma rescue station is planned for Gokyo along with another porter shelter (you are invited to be a part of the project's success, donations accepted at donations@ippg.net).

Enviable viewpoints and side-excursions make Gokyo an attractive destination to enjoy a few days exploring. The overpowering majesty of the lake surrounded by skyscraping goddesses bound in snow will be an unforgettable, Khumbu highlight.

From Gokyo, Cho Oyu (26,906 feet, 8201 m) looms to the north and straddles the border between Nepal and the Tibetan Frontier. It ranks as the world's sixth highest peak and was first scaled in 1954 from the northwest by an Austrian-led expedition.

Side Trip to Gokyo Ri

*The most popular excursion in the Gokyo area is Gokyo Ri, a commanding viewpoint with a staggering panorama. Ascend the ridge to the northwest to the summit lookout point at 17,585 ft/5360 m, nearly 2300 ft/700 m above Gokyo. The uphill trudge takes **2-2½ hours** if you are well acclimatized and the awaiting reward is a feast of frosty peaks on display. The sweeping panorama reveals four of the planet's six highest summits and much more. From the north*

71

working east are Cho Oyu (26,906 feet, 8201 m, world's sixth highest), Everest (29,028 feet, 8848 m, world's highest), Lhotse (27,890 feet, 8501 m, fourth highest), and Makalu (27,765 feet, 8463 m, fifth highest).

The turquoise lake twinkles below and the first two lakes passed on the way in to Gokyo are visible. The vantage of the colossal swath of Nepal's largest glacier, Ngozumba Glacier cutting through the desolate landscape can give quite an impression—perhaps of an icy planet far, far away from earth. Although mornings are typically clearest in the Himalaya, if weather is clear, then the sunset on Everest from her is even better because the angle of lighting will provide more favorable views. This evening show drenches the peaks in robust colors. Bring a flashlight for the long return back down the mountain to a well-deserved hot drink and restful coziness of a lodge.

Side Trip to 4th, 5th and 6th Lakes, including 'Scoundrel's Viewpoint'.

Heading north from **Gokyo**, there is relatively little elevation gain to hike up to at least three more pristine lakes and non-stop mountain views. Follow the trail north between the lateral moraine of Ngozumba Glacier and hills to the west, or follow a more strenuous route along the moraine crest for thrilling views on the way to the fourth lake, **Thonak Tso** (15,860 ft, 4834 m) about ¾–1½ **hours** from Gokyo. The next lake, **Ngozumba Tsho** (16,355 feet, 4985 m), is another **1½ hours**. Climb the crest of the moraine, informally known as 'Scoundrel's Viewpoint,' for an unobstructed panorama, with marvelous views to the east, or climb a few hundred meters up the hill to the north of the lake for a vista that will truly take your breath away of the south face of Cho Oyu. (Climbers can get higher up to Ngozumpa Tse (18,208 feet, 5550 m), with the rewards of an unrivaled panorama of the mountain lover's paradise that surrounds you). To the west are the mesmerizing twin peaks of Cholo (20,003 ft, 6097 m) and Kanchung (19892 ft, 6063 m).

To continue on to the sixth lake, **Gyazumpa Tsho** (16,896 feet, 5150 m), you need to be self-sufficient with camping gear to spend the night or plan for a long day's return to Gokyo. Bring along rations as well as a headlamp in case darkness falls before you make it back. Gyazumpa Tsho lake is reached in **1¼–1¾ more hours**, and offers a superlative viewpoint under the face of Cho Oyo that will be a veritable 'billion star hotel' if you overnight here. Enjoy *the bright stars of the heavens blinking above and the peace and quiet of this celestial venue, the*

exact epicenter of the middle of nowhere.

RETURNING FROM GOKYO

The following are four options for returning from **Gokyo**:

-retrace your steps down the valley to Namche

-retrace as far as Phanka and cross to the serene east side of the valley and travel down to Phortse (or a variation of this east side of the valley hike that first passes through Thangnak).

-alternatively, to head to the foot of Everest, cross the Cho La described above in reverse to reach the Khumbu Glacier and the featured trail to Everest Base Camp at Lobuche.

-Finally, take on the challenging, less-used option of crossing the remote Renjo (aka, Lhenjo) La (17,635 feet, 5375m) to the west and descend into the isolated Bhote Kosi Valley to Thame and on to Namche (described after the route description on the east side of the valley via Phortse).

GOKYO TO NAMCHE (OR PANGBOCHE) VIA PHORTSE

A return to Namche along the east side of the Dudh Kosi Valley includes two options. The first option is the main route along the west side of the valley from **Gokyo** to a junction just before Phangka (10-15 minutes before reaching the lodges). From there, drop down to cross the headwaters of the Dudh Kosi to the lodging of **Na** (14,435 feet, 4400 m), 30 minutes from leaving the main trail **(2 hours from Gokyo).** Na lies in a serene meadow away from the crowds. Continue south and cross a tributary above the valley floor and tie in with the **upper route** from Thangnak in **45 minutes**.

Continue south to the lodging of **Thare** in **30-45 minutes**. Cross a tributary to more lodging of **Thore** in **30-45 more minutes**. In another ¾-1 hour reach herders' **seasonal, stone-built dwellings** and in less than **30 minutes** ascend to a ridge with a *stupa* overlooking **Phortse**. Phortse is another **hour** below this *stupa*, **6-7 hours** from Gokyo.

Gokyo to Phortse via Thangnak

This isolated route is ideal for trekkers looking for a dose of adventure. It is a variation of the east side of the valley route to Phortse; begin by traversing the desolate Ngozumpa Glacier. The trail leads off from the hotels at Gokyo. Do your best to follow previous paths across the glacier and take care around exposed sections of trail. Once across, head south to Thangnak, **1½-2 hours** from **Gokyo**. Follow the stream south and in less than **20 minutes**, stay on the left (northeast) side (right descends to Na) and contour above a stream, passing a seasonal herders' settlement in another **20 minutes**, and more huts in **10-15 more minutes**. Beyond are more stone-built huts and an impressive *stupa* before descending to meet the lower trail from Na in **30 minutes**. Continue south to the lodging of **Thare** in **30-45 minutes**. Cross a tributary to more lodging of **Thore** in **30-45 more minutes**. In **¾-1 hour** reach **more seasonal dwellings** and in less than **30 minutes** ascend to a ridge with a large *stupa* overlooking **Phortse**. Phortse lies **an hour** below this *stupa*, **4-5 hours** from Thangnak.

Phortse is perched on a plateau that lies between the Dudh Kosi and Khumbu River valleys (the Gokyo and Everest Base Camp routes respectively). The distinctive Khumbu village of about 80 homes has a *gomba*, hydropower station and lodging for tourists, and is pleasantly located near a grove of silver birch trees. Phortse is the perfect place to relax, unwind and enjoy a rest day or two after the long hikes on the trails and is one of the best

places in the Khumbu to observe traditional Sherpa lifestyle.

Onward from Phortse, descend for **30 minutes** through a peaceful forest to the west to the Dudh Kosi (11,200 ft/3414 m) and meet the main trail to Namche on the west side of the valley at Phortse Tenga. This route has been described above in reverse in the Namche to Gokyo section. Another option from Phortse is to continue east on a thrilling high traverse with occasional precipitous drop-offs to Upper **Pangboche**, a **2–3-hour** hike. From Pangboche, head back to Namche by way of Tengboche (described perviously in reverse in the section **GORAK SHEP TO PANGBOCHE AND PHORTSE**).

RENJO LA HIGH PASS FROM GOKYO TO THAME

Consider this long day over an isolated high pass only if you are feeling physically fit and fine and looking for an exhilirating adventure. Renjo La (17,634 feet, 5375m) lies to the west of Gokyo and links the Dudh Kosi Valley with the Bhote Kosi Valley. After descending from the pass it follows an ancient trade route to Thame village and on to Namche. Traversing the pass from Gokyo to Lungde makes for a long, strenuous day. Bring snacks for the journey as there are no facilities until Lungde some 5½–

6½ hours away from Gokyo. The path is quite steep as you near the pass itself and, as with other high crossings, it should not be attempted under poor weather conditions and especially after recent snowfall. It should only be attempted if you are well-acclimatized to high elevation.

The trail to Renjo La from Gokyo branches left from the track to Gokyo Ri and follows along the north side of the lake. Relish a continuous banquet of views along the way which reach a zenith at the pass with its jaw-dropping panorama.

Along the way, the path contours around snow and ice and through scree and gets especially steep as you near the pass. Cairns mark the way to **Renjo La, 2¾–3¾ hours** from Gokyo. Take a last gaze at the beautiful turquoise lake beside Gokyo, and on the other side of the pass you are greeted by an emerald lake sparkling below. Descend the other side on a stone-laid path that travels to the south of this lake.

Continue down on a wide path and pass by a few ponds on a relatively gentle slope most of the way to **Lungde** (14,370 feet, 4380 m) with five lodges, **2¼-3¼ hours** from the Renjo La. (For trekkers wishing to prolong the journey a bit and get away from the main route, then north of Lungde up

the Bhote Kosi valley, less than an hour away, is the small settlement of Ariye that sees few foreigners and has lodging, too.)

From Lungde to Thame, descend briefly to where the trail meets the centuries-old trading route that heads north over the Nangpa La (18,750 feet, 5715 m) to the Tibetan Frontier. After the Chinese takeover of Tibet by China in 1950-51, trade on this route was greatly reduced. Nowadays, electronics and consumer goods replace the traditional goods that used to be transported on this route. Most of the tourist trinkets and jewels sold along the Khumbu trailside also come from Tibet by way of this route. **Advisory:** If you are thinking about exploring the pass, please note that the Nangpa La is restricted and under Chinese surveillance. Their border patrol has been known to fire indiscriminately at interlopers who approach the controlled area, foreigners and locals alike.

To continue to Thame, follow downstream along the east side of the Bhote Kosi with Kyajo Ri looming above to the east. **Marlung** (13,812 feet, 4210 m) is **40 minutes away** with teahouses and lodging on both sides of the river (two lodges lie on the northeast side before crossing the Bhote Kosi and two more on the southwest side). To the west above the second set of lodges is a trail that climbs to Chudungbo viewpoint with an inspiring panorama of the snowcapped Himalayan peaks and surrounding territory. Continue on the west bank of the river to the seasonal settlement of **Taranga** in **30–40 minutes** with a lodge and a few tea shops. Traveling on the west bank, pass a sign that indicates a detour to Kyaro Gomba, aka, Kerok Gomba (an inactive monastery claimed by locals to be 400 years old) and begin to encounter signs of the *Thame Environment Trail* (previously described in the Thame section)

before arriving at the magnificent plateau of Thame Teng in **1-1¼ hours**. Thame Teng has one lodge with more under construction. An army outpost is just behind a majestic *stupa* surrounded by *mani* stones. The local version of the prominent Sherpa festival, *Dumchi* takes place at this *stupa* around June every year (other locations for this festival are Namche, Khumjung, Rimijung and Lukla). Reach **Thame** in **less than 30 more minutes**. Thame and the route to Namche have been described previously in the section on side trips from Namche.

MORE SIDE-TOURS IN THE KHUMBU

The Khumbu is a mountain lover's Nirvana, ideal for anyone looking for robust adventure and exploration in the highlands. The four main river valleys have numerous, inviting side valleys. Almost any ridge can be hiked up for a buffet of wondrous views. Some of the options are mentioned in the route descriptions above whereas others await your discovery.

The sacred landscape with continuous mountain scenery makes for an exhilarating trekking odyssey wherever you venture within this expansive wedge of the unforgettable Himalaya!

DUDH KOSI VALLEY TO ARUN VALLEY AND TUMLINGTAR VIA SALPA BHANJYANG

Occasionally, trekkers made the hardscrabble journey into or out of Solu–Khumbu via Tumlingtar in the Arun River valley. This option is an arduous trek, cutting across several river valleys with strenuous ups and downs. Facilities along the way are less developed and the remote route is not always straightforward; travelers sometimes need to ask locally for onward directions. The hike from Solu–Khumbu and the Dudh Kosi valley to the Arun valley begins at Bupsa and is briefly outlined below. Be advised that in November of 2012, there was a wild bear attack in the forests between Bung and Cheskam and five local people were injured.

From **Bupsa**, leave the Dudh Kosi valley trail and climb up to the east to Kharte and Bhalukop. Ascend to the lodges and *gomba* of Pangkom (9338 feet, 2846 m), **2–2½ hours** from Bupsa. You could also reach this village by hiking up the valley to the east of Karikhola village. Continue past the *gomba* up to Pangkom La (10,410 feet, 3173 m), a pass in a rhododendron woodland. The other waypoints along this route are the following:

Shibuche
Surki (Sipki) La
Boksom/Khiraule Gomba
Bung
Gudel
Nimchola, or Share
Sanam
Salpa Bhanjyang
Gurase

Jaubari
Phedi
Dobhane
Gothe
Balawa Besi
Kartikeghat/Kartikepul
Gidhe/Kumal
Tumlingtar

ENTRY PERMITS AND TIMS CARDS

Advisory: If you trek into the Khumbu from the lowlands, obtain a Sagarmatha National Park permit and TIMS card in Kathmandu, and even still, you might be forced to purchase a Gauri-Shankar Conservation Area permit in Shivalaya for passing through the southern fringes of that park.

The Sagarmatha National Park Entry Permit is 3000 NPR and TIMS card is $20 USD equivalent.

NATIONAL PARK AND CONSERVATION AREA entry permits are processed at the National Parks and Conservation office in Bhrikutimandap, Kathmandu, with fees up to 3000 NRS (Nepali rupees) per person, per entry. **Bring your passport or a photocopy and two photographs (plus two more photos for the TIMS card).** Separate charges and supplementary permits are required from the Immigration Department for restricted areas, including: Kangchenjunga, Manaslu, Naar and Phu, Upper Mustang, Dolpo, Shey-Phoksundo, Mugu and Humla.

Documents will be checked at national park and conservation area entry points and often at police check posts along the routes. It is best to obtain permits beforehand to avoid hassles and increased fees **(e.g., the Annapurna Conservation Area Permit fee is double at entry points)**. Checkpoints are useful sources of information on trail updates and advisories. Carry a photocopy of your passport and visa as some police posts request details be written in a logbook.

TREKKER INFORMATION MANAGEMENT SYSTEM (TIMS) CARDS

For the popular trekking destinations, a Trekker Information Management System (TIMS) registration card is to be presented at checkpoints along with conservation area or national park entry permits. For independent trekkers, these TIMS cards are available at a separate TIMS desk at the Nepal Tourism Board (NTB) office in Bhrikutimandap near the counters where national park and conservation area permits are obtained, as well as through trekking agencies and at the offices of the Trekking Agencies' Association of Nepal (TAAN) in Kathmandu (Maligaon) or Pokhara. **A copy of your passport and two passport-sized photos are needed and the equivalent of $20 USD per card for individual trekkers ($10 USD/pax for agency treks, usually taken care of by agencies).**

MOUNTAINEERING

Summary: Among the first foreigners who visited Nepal were mountaineers. Nepal first opened its doors to foreigners in the early 1950s, and they were interested in climbing the highest peaks on the planet. Since then, the Himalaya has become a famous playground and exhilarating outdoor training center for climbers and outdoor enthusiasts alike from around the world.

Nepal boasts ownership or joint-possession of eight of the fourteen tallest peaks of the planet! They make up part of the exclusive group Fourteen Eight Thousanders, or fourteen peaks over 8,000 m (nearly 26,250 ft).

Nepal is home or partially home to the following peaks with height ranking listed first:

1st Everest, 8848 m/29,028 ft
3rd Kanchhenjunga, 8586 m/28,169 ft
4th Lhotse, 8501 m/27,890 ft
5th Makalu, 8463 m/27,765 ft
6th Cho Oyu, 8201 m/26,906 ft
7th Dhaulagiri, 8167 m/26,794 ft
8th Manaslu, 8156 m/26,758 ft
10th Annapurna, 8091 m/26,545 ft

Of these peaks and the fourteen peaks soaring over 8,000 m in the world, Dhaulagiri is the highest peak located entirely within Nepal's borders.

Annapurna I was the first 8,000 m peak to have been climbed. The feat was accomplished by a French-led team in 1950. They had originally recced Dhaulagiri, the world's seventh highest peak. However, they were unable to find a suitable approach route for Dhaulagiri and abandoned it as too challenging and then focused all attention and effort on Annapurna I.

It was not until three years later that Tenzing Norgay Sherpa and Edmund Percival Hillary put Nepal on the map with a feat that thrilled people from around the globe. In May, 1953 they became the first climbers to reach the summit of Everest. Their success was broadcast internationally and brought worldwide media attention to not only the achievement but to Nepal as well. It resulted in a sustained interest in climbing the majestic Himalayan peaks in Nepal, mountains that tower above the lush hill scenery and timeless cultures of the Himalaya.

According to the Nepal Tourism Board, there are 414 peaks in Nepal open for mountaineering. Climbing permits for expedition peaks are issued by the Mountaineering Section of the Ministry of Culture, Tourism and Civil Aviation.

Besides expeditionary peaks, thirty-three minor peaks, or so-called 'trekking summits,' below 6,500 m can be attempted. Permits for these 'trekking summits' are issued by the Nepal Mountaineering Association (NMA), the organization that manages the peaks. Eighteen of these are the original trekking peaks, opened in 1981, and are categorized as Group B. An additional fifteen peaks were added in September 2002 and referred to as Group A peaks. These peaks are challenging and require technical gear and know-how as well as a certified guide. They are named 'trekking peaks' simply because most of them are near trekking routes and easily accessible. Island Peak (aka, *Imja Tse*), is the most popular of these peaks and the most climbed peak in Nepal.

While the Himalayas attract adventurous foreign climbers, the guardian of the Himalaya, the Sherpa, have become the most trusted climbing partners and are often referred to as the *Tigers of the Snow*. Sherpa have long been associated with the mountains that they consider sacred. Their homes in the highlands of the Khumbu make them naturally acclimatized and fit for journeys into the higher elevations up to the peak summits. Most expeditions into Nepal's Himalaya and nowadays, even many outside Nepal are led by Sherpa guides and assistants.

Expeditions in Nepal tend to focus on the highest peaks, but many others peaks are popular as well, including Ama Dablam (6812 m), one of the most elegant peaks in Nepal, often referred to as the *Matterhorn of the Himalaya*. Regardless of height and technical difficulty an attempt on a Himalayan peak with experienced, highly qualified teams led by Sherpa, success is often assured and a lifetime highlight achieved!

Mountaineering in Nepal requires special permits and fees. Climbing permits for expedition peaks are issued by the Mountaineering Section of the Ministry of Culture, Tourism and Civil Aviation.

Besides expeditionary peaks, thirty-three minor peaks, so-called **'Trekking Summits'**, can be attempted. Please see the next section for more information about these peaks.

TREKKING PEAKS

Summary: There are 33 Trekking Peaks that have been opened in Nepal as special climbing adventures. These thrilling summits offer a chance to summit a Himalayan peak with little to no previous mountaineering experience and can be conveniently combined with a standard trek. These 33 peaks offer the chance of a lifetime highlight -- climbing in the Himalaya!

Nepal's 33 Trekking Summits are less than 6,500 m and therefore, take less time and are more affordable than climbing on their higher neighbors. For adventurous people and mountaineers not ready for Nepal's highest peaks requiring expedition style arrangements with months of planning, these 33 exciting peaks offer a chance to climb in the highest playground on the planet, the Himalaya. At the very least, they will spice up a holiday in the Himalaya with a real adventure!

Although these peaks are smaller relative to some of their towering neighbors, these 33 peaks are very high compared to the rest of the world --higher than most of the planet's tallest mountains beyond the Himalayan Range. They are open to adventurous travelers looking for an exhilarating challenge even without previous experience or skills. Many of these peaks can be climbed with a brief training in necessary minimal skills just before the climb.

The majority of these peaks are situated nearby the famous trekking regions of Nepal of Annapurna, Everest, and Langtang and a few are outside of these areas, too, in more remote sections. An attempt on a Trekking Summit can be made as a side excursion to your trekking route and will be often be the trip's most memorable highlight.

Despite the word 'trekking' in the name Trekking Summits, most of these peaks are by no means straightforward. Peak climbing in the Himalaya is full of adventure that requires not only physical and mental stamina and will-power but technical skills and experience. Additionally, special permits are required and issued by the Nepal Mountaineering Association (NMA), the organization that manages these peaks. Moreover, an experienced guide is compulsory and technical gear and alpine clothing is necessary, too. Some of these peaks are difficult and dangerous, and have had only had a few ascents.

Eighteen of these are the original trekking peaks, opened in 1981, and are categorized as **Group B**. An additional fifteen peaks were added in September 2002 and referred to as **Group A** peaks. Detailed, information on the eighteen Group B climbs is available in Bill O'Connor's book *The Trekking Peaks of Nepal*. Island Peak (aka, *Imja Tse*), in the Khumbu is the most popular of these peaks and the most climbed peak in Nepal.

Exploring the greatest mountains in the world is ideal for travelers looking for a more extreme adventure while visiting Nepal. The best seasons to climb in Nepal are March to May and September to early December. Summiting a Himalayan peak can fulfill mountain dreams and strengthen mountain skills for further exploits, perhaps on a higher peak. The extraordinary views from the top of a Himalayan peak are unforgettable and the photos, memories and stories you take home will regale family, friends, and co-workers for a long time to come.

The following Trekking Peaks are in the Khumbu region and adjoining Rolwaling region to the west of Khumbu (the numbers immediately to the right of the peak names indicates the number of climbers in 2012):

Khumbu Himal
Group A
Abi-0 (20,003 feet, 6097 m)
Chhukung Ri-25 (18,238 feet, 5559 m)
Cholatse-19 (21,129 feet, 6440 m)
Kyajo Ri-38 (20,295 feet, 6186 m)
Lobuche West-7 (20,161 feet, 6145 m)
Macchermo-4 (20,463 feet, 6237 m)
Nirekha-16 (19,898 feet, 6065 m)
Ombigaichen-0 (20801 feet, 6340 m)
Phari Lapcha-0 (19,741 feet, 6017 m)

Group B
Imja Tse-6,010 (Island Peak) (20,210 feet, 6160 m)
Khongma Tse-21 (19,094 feet, 5820 m)
Kusum Kanguru-17 (20,889 feet, 6367 m)
Kwangde-12 (19,721 feet, 6011 m)
Lobuche East-1202 (20,075 feet, 6119 m)
Mera Peak-2,972 (21,247 feet, 6476 m)
Pokalde-224 (19,048 feet, 5806 m)

Rolwaling Himal
Group A
Chekijo-3 (20,528 feet, 6257 m)

Group B
Pharchamo-527 (20,299 feet, 6187 m)
Ramdung-120 (19,439 feet, 5925 m)

STAYING HEALTHY

Summary: The main health concerns for tourists traveling in the Himalaya are digestive issues, aka traveler's tummy, respiratory problems (sometimes known as the Khumbu cough) and environmental challenges of altitude sickness, keeping well-fed, hydrated and warm. The rewards of being physically prepared and staying healthy are many and make for much greater enjoyment of Nepal's natural wonders including eight the world's top ten highest peaks.

Traveling safely and comfortably in the Himalaya is the ideal but that depends on several external factors including weather, terrain and facilities, and food and drink as much as on your own preparedness, gear, fitness, and acclimatization. Taking the time to allow for rest and acclimatization during a journey along the world's highest trekking trails will greatly enhance the overall experience. In order to assist your overall well-being, you might consider hiring porters to help carry the load. While some trekkers resist the idea, by employing a porter, you will not only allow yourself more energy for the trails but more freedom to witness and enjoy the natural splendor on a trip of a lifetime in the Himalaya. At the same time, you will be providing an income with better pay than most jobs in the region. Porters and guides often provide cultural insights and you might each end up with a newfound friend.

In the Khumbu, be prepared for cold winds and possibly snow, and temperatures below freezing, especially overnight. Moreover, it is critical to heed the warning signs of altitude sickness described below. Not a few people have died in this region from acute mountain sickness, and it cannot not be underestimated.

That said, gastro-intestinal issues and respiratory infections are the primary causes of illness in travelers to Nepal, and slips from the trail are the leading cause of death to trekkers. Trail safety should not be overlooked among other concerns. Difficult conditions might be encountered at high elevations far from help. Unexpected weather can arrive swiftly and without warning. Consider obtaining travel and evacuation insurance in addition to standard medical coverage.

A useful health information resource is the US Center for Disease Control's country-specific website for Nepal, http://wwwnc.cdc.gov/travel/destinations/traveler/none/nepal.

THE TREKKER'S PERSONAL FIRST-AID KIT

- **Altitude Medicine** Acetazolamide (Diamox), 250-mg tablets
- **Antibiotics**, e.g., azithromycin, ciprofloxacin or norfloxacin (broad spectrum, especially useful for bacterial diarrhea and other infections)
- **Anti-fungal cream**
- **Antihistamine/decongestant** for colds and allergies
- **Anti-motility medicine** loperamide (2 mg) for unavoidable travel while suffering with diarrhea
- **Antiseptic** for cleaning wounds, e.g., Betadine
- **Band-aids**
- **Elastic Bandages/Gauze Pads**
- **Moleskin, Secondskin, Blister Pads** Felt or foam for the prevention of blisters
- **Motion Sickness tablets** for vehicle travel
- **Oral rehydration powder** aka, *Jeevan Jal*, can be purchased in pharmacy shops, health posts, and general shops
- **Painkiller, anti-inflammatory, anti-fever tablets**
- **Sunscreen** ayurvedic sun block creams are available in Kathmandu
- **Throat lozenges**
- **Temporary filling material** for dental emergencies and/or eugenol, oil of cloves, used as a topical analgesic and antiseptic
- **Tinidazole** for *giardiasis* and *amoebiasis* (protozoan infections)
- **Water purification materials** (see below)

DIARRHEA

The CIWEC website has an informative web page for visitors to Nepal, "Understanding Diarrhea in Travelers" at http://ciwec-clinic.com/health-information/understanding-diarrhea-in-travelers/

Bacterial infection is the most common cause of travelers' diarrhea in Nepal. Symptoms generally include quick onset accompanied or preceded by chills or fever and cramps. **Ciprofloxacin**, 500-mg, is the antibiotic of choice for infectious bacterial illnesses. The dose is one capsule every twelve hours until symptoms subside. Alternatively, **norfloxacin** may be tried, one 400-mg capsule taken every twelve hours until symptoms subside. **Azithromycin** is another good choice. The adult dosage for azithromycin is 500 mg, one capsule per day.

Giardia is the cause of about one in ten cases of travelers presenting with diarrhea at CIWEC. It generally takes a longer time to acquire than bacterial infections, usually two weeks and sometimes longer, after ingesting cysts. Stools often contain mucus and, as with some bacterial cases, might smell like rotten eggs or sulfur, as will expelled gas. A churning stomach, cramping, and bloating are common, vomiting and fever are rare. The treatment is 2 grams of tinidazole as a single dose, repeated in 24 hours.

Cyclospora is a protozoan parasite acquired through contaminated food or drink. Risk of infection is mainly during the monsoon season, June through September. Common symptoms include watery diarrhea, bloating, gas, loss of appetite, and prolonged fatigue. Vomiting, fever, and other flu-like symptoms might present, although some infected people might be asymptomatic. Without medical intervention, the illness might self-limit within a few days to a month or longer, and relapses can occur. Treatment is co-trimoxazole (TMP/SMX) every twelve hours for seven days. *Cyclospora* cysts are resistant to disinfectants and can survive chlorine and iodine, which then leaves boiling as the surest means of purifying water.

WATER PURIFICATION

Although boiling is the safest means to treat drinking water, it is not usually feasible and requires scarce fuel resources, especially in rural areas. Bottled water is available on popular treks but will be difficult to find on trails that see few tourists. It is claimed to be treated, although studies repeatedly find contaminated supplies. Disposal of empty bottles is burdensome to the environment, too. Using a filter, even a piece of clean cloth, is a good idea as most microorganisms are not free floating but attached to particles in water. Means of treating water while traveling include the following:

Chlorine Dioxide **droplets or tablets**, though not easily found in Nepal, are better than other chorine-based options available in Kathmandu, which do not offer full protection.

Troclosene sodium (sodium dicholoroisocyanurate), chlorine disinfectant now widely available in Kathmandu under different names including **Aquatabs** and **Micropure**.

Iodine Tablets, use one tablet per quart (liter) of water. Available in Kathmandu at KEEP and elsewhere.

Tincture of Iodine (**USP – United States Pharmacopeia),** 2% solution. Add five drops per quart (liter), wait 30 minutes before drinking

Strong Iodine Solution (**BP - British Pharmacopeia),** 10% solution, one-two drops and wait 30 minutes

Lugol's Solution (iodine), available in some pharmacies in Kathmandu as well as the larger stores that cater to wealthier clientele. Solution strength may vary; if 2% solution, then 4-5 drops per quart (liter).

Filtering, water filters are effective but bulky to carry.

UV Light (SteriPEN), small handheld device with reputed ability to purify a liter of clear water in less than 2 minutes. Requires expensive batteries. Devices are available in Kathmandu at KEEP and some trekking supply shops. Don't depend on it without a backup system.

Drink mixes can be added to improve flavor to chemically treated water *after* the disinfection period has elapsed.

Food Hygiene

Food contamination might occur from the preparation and handling of the food by unclean hands (hand soap is not widely used in Nepal), unclean plates, cups and utensils, flies and airborne contaminants. Be vigilant but realize that lack of complete sanitation is a fact of life in Nepal and comes with the territory. Food can otherwise be assumed to be safe if it has just been cooked and not left out for a long period of time.

Dining and Drinking Nepali Style

Summary: Travelers in Nepal can choose from local food, typically dal-bhat-tarakari (rice, lentil soup and a vegetable dish, and sometimes roti, a flatbread, is substituted for rice), to regional and beyond. Dal-bhat-tarakari uses local resources and is often the freshest and best choice on the menu for a quality, satisfying meal. In the Khumbu, shyakpa stew is a Sherpa favourite -- bowl of handmade noodles with potatoes and other seasonal vegetables, tsampa (buckwheat or barley flour mixed with hot water or solja, salt-butter tea, with perhaps a side of lentils or vegetables and eaten as a doughy paste), potatoes (in many variations) and westernized dishes.

While trekking, for a greater cultural experience, do your best to dine and drink Nepali style and choose the same food as your hosts. Not only while you be supporting their farms, but you will be eating the freshest items available. The typical Nepali dish is *dal-bhat-tarakari* -- *a heaping plate of* rice, lentil soup and vegetables. Although consisting of the same general ingredients, this dish has a wide range of tastes depending on the vegetables, seasonings and preparation from place to place (and even day to day at the same location). Unlimited quantities of rice are generally included in the meal, and sometimes flatbread is substituted, but the lentil soup and vegetables are rationed. In the commercialized trekking areas, second helpings of each might be offered but not more and might be charged extra. The custom is to have this meal freshly prepared, and often quantities are misjudged prior to preparation for large groups and extra helpings then might not be available. Another option in the hills is *dhirdo* (corn, millet, or buckwheat mash served with lentil soup and vegetables).

Busy trailside hotels often offer extensive 'international' menus with a wide variety of dishes. As much as possible, try to avoid packaged foods. Although quick-cooking, packaged noodles have become more commonplace throughout much of the country, they are usually insufficient as a meal replacement (nutritionally and size-wise), and contain MSG and animal by-products. Often the plastic packaging is tossed aside indiscriminately or burned and adds to pollution problems that locals do not know how to deal with adequately. Travelers are encouraged to eat local food which is what the lodge owners and staff usually eat, too. Dining and drinking Nepali style is not only delicious but more energy-efficient and better all-around for the environment.

Fresh fruit can be hard to come by in the hills and is rarely available in the alpine heights. Regular, weekly markets occur in some villages and are a source of occasional fruits and other fresh products, general supplies and entertainment, too.

Western processed and packaged foods are available in large 'supermarkets' in Kathmandu that cater mainly to tourists, expatriates and wealthy Nepalese. You may want to bring dried fruit and nuts as a trail supplement, and combined with chocolate, it makes for a tasty snack. Sealable containers are convenient to carry snacks, too.

Tea with milk and sugar is the traditional Nepali beverage called *chiyaa*. Lodge owners along popular routes will make it without milk or sugar on request. In higher territory, Tibetan salt-butter tea is available, although it is an acquired taste and takes a while to get used to. Other than tea, you might simply ask for boiled water to replenish your fluids, and even carry your own favorite tea with you.

Local alcoholic drinks include *chyang and roxy* and *tongba* and are essential for entertaining guests!

Chyang is fermented but not distilled while **roxy** is distilled. These drinks are usually made from locally grown millet, rice or maize. **Tongba** is a drink made by pouring hot water into a container of fermented millet and the liquid is sipped through a bamboo or aluminum straw. Commercially bottled alcohol is available at higher prices.

The type of food and drink available on the trekking trails varies depending on the place and the season. Try dining and drinking Nepali style and you will be getting not just better value for your money but a much closer experience of Himalayan lifestyle. *A favorite local saying, 'dal-bhat power, 24 hours!'...it might not be quite 24 hours of food energy but it does keep you going strong.*

If you would like to splurge for a day, five-star hotels regularly host all you can eat buffets that include access to swimming pools and luxurious surroundings.

Respiratory Infections

Upper-respiratory infections, including the common cold occur frequently in Nepal. Physicians in the high-altitude Khumbu region have noted that the three most common ailments there are **bronchitis**, aka, "*Khumbu cough*," brought on by cold, arid conditions, **gastroenteritis**, and **viral upper-respiratory infections**.

ALTITUDE ILLNESS AND ENVIRONMENT-INDUCED HEALTH PROBLEMS

While trekking in the lap of the highest mountains on Earth, certain precautions are necessary. Visitors must pay heed to the environment and to messages their own bodies are giving as well as signs that fellow travelers might be in need of assistance. Information sessions about altitude illness are given by the Himalayan Rescue Association in Kathmandu and at aid posts in the Khumbu at **Pheriche** and **Maccherma** and in the Annapurna Region at **Manang**. (Additional information on altitude illness is available from CIWEC at http://ciwec-clinic.com/health-information/altitude-illness-advice-for-the-trekker)

Physically fit, active people might be at increased risk given that their increased strength, stamina and vitality might allow them to ascend more quickly with relative ease and athletes might also be accustomed to pushing through pain and discomfort, especially dangerous at elevation. Altitude illness can strike regardless of fitness level and is prevented by proper acclimatization, ascending gradually while allowing rest days and being watchful of symptoms. **Acetazolamide** (Diamox) is beneficial in helping the acclimatization process, too. The preventative dose is 125 mg two to three times a day, begun a day before ascending to higher elevations, and can be increased to 250 mg when symptoms present. (For more reading, **Travel at High Altitude** can be downloaded for free at www.medex.org.uk).

If any of the following **mild Acute Mountain Sickness (AMS)** symptoms are present, then do not ascend higher but remain at the current elevation or descend until better. If symptoms worsen, descend to below the elevation where symptoms arose and **DO NOT ASCEND HIGHER:**

- **headache**
- **nausea**
- **loss of appetite**
- **difficulty sleeping**
- **fatigue**
- **dizziness or light-headedness**

Serious symptoms of altitude illness require immediate descent without delay, regardless of hour and by porter, pack animal or other means if necessary. These symptoms include:

- **lack of balance, loss of coordination, staggering, inability to walk a straight line (this is the most serious indicator of altitude sickness and requires immediate descent)**
- **breathlessness at rest, difficulty breathing**
- **mental confusion**
- **severe headache**
- **rapid resting heart rate—120 or more beats per minute**
- **persistent cough, coughing up fluid**
- **blueness of face and lips**
- **persistent vomiting**

Frostbite (frozen body tissues) is rare in trekkers. Prevent cold injuries with adequate clothing (donning and doffing layers as needed; wet clothing is especially dangerous at altitude where temperatures can drop quickly and precipitously) and equipment, by eating enough food, and by avoiding dehydration and exhaustion. (Conversely, to counter hot weather, soaking bandannas, hats, and shirts in water and then wearing the wet clothing can be helpful, too.)

SAFETY IN THE HIMALAYA

Summary: Compared to the rest of the world, Nepal is a relatively safe place to travel. The kindhearted people cherish visitors and are welcoming and hospitable. However, dangers do still exist and trekkers have gone missing (do not travel alone!) but physical assault is rare. Falls on the footpaths are a leading cause of concern. Take care while you enjoy the most magnificent trails of the world, endowed with all the glory of the Himalaya.

Travel in Nepal is relatively much safer than most modernized countries although lawlessness is on the rise, particularly in the southern plains, due to a weak central government. Of the less than 1000 cases filed by tourists yearly with the Tourist Police, over 80% are for theft. However, there are instances of intimidation, assaults and harassment, and foreigners have gone missing. Rare attacks on trekkers have occurred in remote areas and usually to lone travelers. Do not trek alone, especially on lesser-used routes, and especially as a female (unfortunately, double standards exist).

Find a trustworthy travel companion or hire a guide and porter. Sexual harassment is not uncommon. Lurid foreign media is mis-attributed to all foreigners. Dressing as conservatively as Nepalis will gain cultural acceptance. Female travelers and families with children might be especially interested in hiring female crew and doing so also helps women in Nepal to improve their socio-economic situation in a land with a shortage of opportunities for females. If you hire a porter, bring a small lock for security of your bags while they are away from you to prevent possible pilfering and recriminations. Small locks and cheap duffel bags are available in Kathmandu.

Bear in mind, difficult conditions might be encountered at high elevations far from help. Unexpected weather can arrive swiftly. Nepal aims to provide secondary health care in each of the 75 districts with hospitals staffed by physicians. Primary health care is provided by health posts scattered throughout each district. If an emergency occurs, local schoolteachers may be a helpful resource and usually can speak English.

Trail safety in the Himalaya should not be overlooked among other risks, and slips from the trail are the leading cause of injury to trekkers. Consider obtaining travel and evacuation insurance in addition to standard medical coverage. The Himalayan Rescue Association might help arrange insurance in Kathmandu as well as the Nepal Mountaineering Association. The Himalayan Rescue Association (HRA) reports that Nepal has over 150 helicopter evacuations annually. The cost of helicopter rescue is high—nearly $2,500 per hour and companies charge a minimum of three hours for round trip rescue flights from Kathmandu to the Annapurna and Everest regions. The phone numbers of your trekking agency, embassy and rescue operators should be checked once you reach Kathmandu and kept with you while trekking.

Vehicle safety is another issue for tourists in Nepal as road traffic can be chaotic. Night travel in general is not recommended for safety and comfort. At all times keep your limbs and head inside the moving vehicles and not hanging out a window because the passing of other automobiles and roadside objects can be harrowingly close. While traveling, be aware that packs and luggage left unattended might be targeted by thieves. Locks are useful and it is best to keep easily removed items deep inside your bag. During stops, it is safest to bring carry-on items and all valuables with you.

Of dangers and safety in the Himalaya, earthquakes are a leading concern. A 2001 study listed Kathmandu as the world's most earthquake-vulnerable city, and the country is in a seismically active zone. In fact, it is the collision of the Indo-Australian Plate and the Eurasian Plate that led to the uprising of the world's highest range and one of earth's greatest natural spectacles, the Himalaya. The 2001 study focused on the following three criteria: building frailty, potential for landslides and floods, and the capability of local authorities for rescue, firefighting, and life-saving operations. Preparedness has improved little since 2001, while population density has only increased.

Register with your embassy upon arrival and make copies of your passport and visa and other valuable documents in the unlikely event you will need replacements. Save important details including contact info by email or other electronic accounts.

If you take care of your safety in the Himalaya, everything else will fall into place and your journey in this captivating land will be a pleasant highlight of a lifetime!

TRAVEL AND EVACUATION INSURANCE

Summary: Traveling the wonders of the Himalaya including the highest mountains on earth, has inherent risks and dangers. Nepal's terrain is steep and passes through remote territory. Weather can also change unexpectedly causing additional hazards. Consider obtaining travel and evacuation insurance in addition to standard medical coverage.

Nepal is a nature lover's paradise and adventure opportunities abound. Nowadays, in addition to trekking, tourists can enjoy canyoning, rafting, bungee jumping, paragliding, mountain biking, jungle safaris and more.

Along with the enjoyment of the great outdoors and a growing choice of adventure activities, certain risks are encountered. There are dangers inherent in activities in the mountains, rivers and jungles which are often remote and away from services found in cities. Although facilities and services are continually improving and Nepal is enjoying greater development in all sectors, the hazards of adventure in this land, rich with nature's wealth should not be overlooked.

Visitors will want to consider obtaining travel and evacuation insurance in the event it is needed. Chances are that everything will be fine as Nepalese guides are some of the best and most experienced in the world, however, Mother Nature occasionally has a stronger say in the matter.

Having travel and evacuation insurance might not keep you at the time of need from having to arrange payment for helicopter rescue should it be necessary. It will help to recover costs. The Himalayan Rescue Association (HRA) reports that Nepal has over 150 helicopter evacuations annually. The cost of helicopter evacuation is high—nearly $2,500 per hour and companies charge a minimum of three hours for round trip rescue flights from Kathmandu to the Annapurna and Everest regions. This has to be underwritten by the party involved, unless rescue insurance has been taken out previously; alpine clubs in your home country sometimes provide insurance as will some organizations in Nepal. The Himalayan Rescue Association might help arrange insurance in Kathmandu as well as the Nepal Mountaineering Association.

Pheriche (Everest) rescues are coordinated by HRA's Mr. Basyal +977 9841320378, and 038-540214 and Manang (Annapurna) by HRA's Mr. Acharya +977 9841355667 and +977 993664515. Register at your embassy in Kathmandu to facilitate the process in the event they receive a rescue message.

If air rescue and evacuation is necessary, send a message to Kathmandu for a helicopter. City area codes are 01 for Kathmandu and 061 for Pokhara (you may have to omit the initial zero depending on from where the call is made). The phone numbers of the agencies and rescue facilities should be checked once you reach Kathmandu. Phone numbers change frequently. There is no emergency network in Nepal. You can try the police emergency numbers 100, 110, and 122. Rescue messages should be sent to one or more of the following:

• **Himalayan Rescue Association** (tel. 01-4440292, and 4440293, mobile +977 9851033046, hra@mail.com.np, www.himalayanrescue.org)
• **The embassy or consulate of the person in need**
• **The trekking agency that organized the trek**, if applicable; (obtain the personal number of the managing director before you depart Kathmandu)

Helicopter Operators
• Fishtail Air (tel. 01-4112217, 4112230; mobile, +977 9751000120, 9851026185)
• Mountain Helicopters (tel. 01-4111031; fax : 01-4111049; mobile, +977 9751020015)
• Air Dynasty Heli-Services (tel. 01-4497418, 4477562; fax,01- 4468802; mobile, +977 9851030013)
• Simrik Air (tel. 01-4155340)
• Nepalese Army (tel. 01-4246140, 01-4246932, 01-4241731, fax 977-1-4269624)
• Manang Air (tel. 01-4496253)
• Shree Airlines (tel. 01-4220172)

Nepal aims to provide secondary health care in each of the 75 districts with hospitals staffed by physicians. Primary health care is provided by health posts scattered throughout each district. If an emergency occurs, then contact the nearest local school teachers who are usually helpful and can speak some English. It is recommended that guides, porters and other staff that you hire be provided with the same standard of medical care as you would expect for yourself. Good-speed and enjoy your travels!

EMERGENCY CARE AND RESCUE FACILITIES

Nepal aims to provide secondary health care in each of the 75 districts with hospitals staffed by physicians. Primary health care is provided by health posts scattered throughout each district. If an emergency occurs, local schoolteachers may be a helpful resource and usually can speak English.

Additionally, keep in mind that a main reason behind a TIMS card charge is to provide rescue funds for trekkers and staff. It may be a challenge convincing TAAN and NTB to reimburse you, however, rescue is a service they consented to when implementing TIMS card fees, and there ought to be a large reserve of funds for this given the amount of funds they have collected from tourists.

HELICOPTER RESCUE

The Himalayan Rescue Association (HRA) reports that Nepal has over 150 helicopter evacuations annually. The cost of helicopter rescue is high—nearly $2,500 per hour and companies charge a minimum of three hours for round trip rescue flights from Kathmandu to the Annapurna and Everest regions. This has to be underwritten by the party involved, unless rescue insurance has been taken out previously; consider supplemental coverage in addition to standard insurance. Alpine clubs in your home country sometimes provide insurance as will some organizations in Nepal. HRA www.himalayanrescue.org, and NMA www.nepalmountaineering.org might have more information on registered agencies in Kathmandu.

Pheriche (Everest) rescues are coordinated by HRA's Mr. Basyal +977 9841320378, and 038-540214 and Manang (Annapurna) by HRA's Mr. Acharya +977 9841355667 and +977 993664515. Register at your embassy in Kathmandu to facilitate the process in the event they receive a rescue message.

EMERGENCY PHONE NUMBERS

If air rescue is necessary, send a message to Kathmandu for a helicopter. City area codes are 01 for Kathmandu and 061 for Pokhara (you might have to omit the zero depending on from where the call is made). The phone numbers of your trekking agency and rescue facilities should be kept handy and checked once you reach Kathmandu. Phone numbers change frequently. There is no emergency network in Nepal. You can try the police emergency numbers 100, 110, and 122. Rescue messages should be sent to one or more of the following (redundancy helps ensure that at least one message will get through) in order of preference:

• **Himalayan Rescue Association** (tel. 01-4440292, and 4440293, mobile +977 9851033046, hra@mail.com.np, www.himalayanrescue.org)
• **The embassy or consulate of the victim** (for U.S., tel. 01-4007200, 01-4007266, 01-4007269, fax 01-400-7281, http://nepal.usembassy.gov; for Canada, tel. 01-4415193; for U.K., tel. 01-4410583; for Australia, tel. 01-4371678)
• **The trekking agency that organized the trek**, if applicable; (get the home phone number of the managing director before you leave Kathmandu)

Helicopter Operators
• Fishtail Air (tel. 01-4112217, 4112230; mobile, +977 9751000120, 9851026185)
• Mountain Helicopters (tel. 01-4111031; fax : 01-4111049; mobile, +977 9751020015)
• Air Dynasty Heli-Services (tel. 01-4497418, 4477562; fax,01- 4468802; mobile, +977 9851030013)
• Simrik Air (tel. 01-4155340)
• Nepalese Army (tel. 01-4246140, 01-4246932, 01-4241731, fax 977-1-4269624)
• Manang Air (tel. 01-4496253)
• Shree Airlines (tel. 01-4220172)

INDEPENDENT TREKKING

On the popular routes, your main contacts will likely be with other trekkers. If you do not have a partner, then it is relatively easy to join up with other trekkers in Kathmandu. People post for trekking partners on bulletin boards at the Kathmandu Environmental Education Project (KEEP) office and in tourist-frequented places like cafes and hotels in Thamel, Kathmandu and Lakeside, Pokhara. The following website might also be helpful: http://trekkingpartners.com/ads/nepal although it has become quite commercial.

Unfortunately, double standards are prevalent, and women especially should not travel alone and are advised to seek out a trekking partner or a female guide or porter (Venus Treks and Tours, www.venustreks.com , can assist with arrangements). Nepalese find it difficult to understand why foreigners, especially women, would travel alone as most Nepalis do not. Although the same goes for men, it is not uncommon to see Nepali men traveling alone if necessary.

GUIDES AND PORTERS

An informed guide can make all the difference on your adventure in the Himalaya. A guide will keep you on the correct course, show you the side-routes, and will assist in other ways, too. He or she will share a wealth of knowledge and insight on the land, route highlights, culture, traditions and more and will assist in arranging food and accommodation and other logistics. A guide will generally ensure your well-being and allow you the greater chance to experience all of Nepal's highlights and attractions.

Traveling with a porter, hired to carry a load, can also be a tremendous opportunity to get to know Nepal and its people, culture and lifestyle. If you are uncomfortable with the idea of allowing another person to carry your own gear, then keep in mind, employment is cherished here in an employment-starved country.

Having a porter is a mutually beneficial arrangement, providing a decent wage, better than most other jobs available, and it will allow more freedom and ease to enjoy the journey and the cultural and natural attractions along the way. Even if you do not hire a porter, you will be an indirect recipient of porter labor whenever you take food and goods along routes and use services built from the materials they hauled. Hiring someone to carry gear will likely be a large pay increase for them over hauling other items for shopkeepers and lodge owners on the trails.

Porters use a conical basket called a *Doko* and seen throughout Nepal. The open top can be covered by plastic to keep the load dry when it rains. *Doko* are carried by a wide band that goes around the forehead called a *naamlo*. Even with a modern pack to carry, most porters prefer the *Doko*. They disregard the pack straps and waist belt in favor of using a *Doko* and tumpline. Items carried by porters often receive rough treatment. It is best to carry the more fragile items yourself along with personal necessities including a water bottle. It would be wise to lock all bags carried by porters to prevent pilfering and recriminations. Small locks and cheap duffel bags are available in Kathmandu.

Be aware that there are instances where a guide (and sometimes a porter) reduces the freedom of movement and choice among lodges, schedules, overnight points, and more. Sometimes, guides receive a small commission for bringing trekkers to lodges and restaurants and become insistent about patronizing those establishments. This can result in disagreements between the guide and guest. It is important to set out guidelines before travel begins, including not only wage, but whether that wage includes food and lodging, and whether the guest or the guide decides on the particular lodge and restaurant and the extent and limitations of the daily schedule. Generally, at teashops, lodges and restaurants, there is a two-tiered pricing system and Nepalis receive a cut rate for rooms and food. However, you will want to set a limit for the daily costs if you are covering them.

The pay rate for guides and porters varies depending on where they are hired, the destination, the time of year, experience and language capabilities and whether the trekker provides food. It is best to have a guide who is actually from the specific area that you will be visiting. Find out current rates for guides and porters from the Kathmandu Environmental Education Project (KEEP) and from other trekkers, and inquire at trekking supply shops and agencies, too. Independently hired guides usually ask and porters will ask for the moon but are open to bargaining. Costs will begin at least 25 percent higher if going through an agency, and the porters and guides will receive appreciably less than if hired directly. However, the Trekking Agents Association of Nepal, is trying to restrict freelance guides and porters and you might then have to go through an agency.

It is also important that porters and guides have adequate clothing for the conditions, elevations and temperatures that will be encountered. KEEP's clothing bank can help with this. All transportation costs such as bus and plane fare to the actual beginning of the trek are the responsibility of the trekker. In addition, if the trek does not leave an employee at his home or point of hiring, the hirer is obligated to pay for his return, usually at half the daily rate. Travel is faster on the return trip, so the number of days the journey will take should be agreed upon in advance.

You can enrich your experience of Nepal's many attractions by employing local guides and porters, whether found on the way or in Kathmandu and Pokhara before beginning your journey. You can also get along just fine on the main routes without assistance. Regardless, please do not trek alone but find a partner for safety reasons. All the best for an enjoyable trek!

NEPALESE PORTER: TOUGH, PROUD, VULNERABLE

(This section is contributed by Dr. Jim Duff, M.D.)

Literally thousands of porters carry loads for trekkers in Nepal every season, either directly for independent trekkers or trekking companies, or indirectly by supplying trekkers' lodges. In addition they carry loads to expedition base camps. These subsistence farmers are usually not from the tiny and famous ethnic group the Sherpa, but are from the valleys of the middle hills. As a result they are not acclimatized to high altitude, and are less aware of the dangers of altitude illness and hypothermia than most trekkers. In caste-conscious Nepal, porters are at the bottom of the pile, and this has led to their neglect and exploitation by their fellow countrymen. It is estimated that several porters still die from preventable causes each year in Nepal despite improvement in their conditions of work over recent years. If you are employing porters, it is vital that you provide them with appropriate clothing and footwear for the altitude and season. Traditionally porters have fended for themselves in terms of food and shelter, but this becomes problematic when there are no villages and lodges are crowded with trekkers; make sure your porters have decent shelter and food.

Trekking agencies are in cutthroat competition for your business, and it is the porters who suffer most from price-cutting. The middleman, guide, or sirdar will often take a cut of their wages and any tip of cash or gear you might leave at the end of your trek. The only way to counter this is to witness or handle these transactions personally. "Overloading" is a new concept to porters who traditionally carried as much as they could possibly manage. While unavoidable in some situations, overloading is generally dangerous, exploitative, and reduces the number of jobs available. In Nepal 65 pounds (30 kg) is considered reasonable and is the legal maximum. Before signing up with a trekking agency, ask about their policy on porter clothing, food, shelter, and wages, and complain if you see any mistreatment while up in the mountains and on return. IPPG (International Porter Protection Group) recommends the following guidelines:

1. Clothing appropriate to season and altitude must be provided to porters for protection from cold, rain, and snow. This may mean: windproof jacket and trousers, fleece jacket, long johns, suitable footwear (boots in snow), socks, hat, gloves, and sunglasses. (KEEP in Kesar Mahal, Thamel, Kathmandu, has a clothing bank where the above items can be borrowed for porters' use and garment and gear donations are accepted, too)

2. *Above the tree line porters should have a dedicated shelter, either a room in a lodge or a tent (the trekkers' mess tent is no good as it is not available till late evening), a sleeping mat, and a decent blanket or sleeping bag. They should be provided with food and warm drinks, or cooking equipment and fuel.*

3. *Porters should be provided with life insurance and the same standard of medical care as you would expect for yourself.*

4. *Porters should not be paid off because of illness/injury without the leader or the trekkers assessing their condition carefully. The person (sirdar) in charge of the porters must let their trek leader or the trekkers know if a sick porter is about to be paid off. Failure to do this has resulted in many deaths. Sick/injured porters should never be sent down alone, but with someone who speaks their language and understands their problem, along with a letter describing their complaint. Sufficient funds should be provided to cover cost of rescue and treatment.*

5. *No porter should be asked to carry a load that is too heavy for their physical abilities (maximum: 20 kg on Kilimanjaro, 25 kg in Peru and Pakistan, 30 kg in Nepal). Weight limits may need to be adjusted for altitude, trail, and weather conditions; experience is needed to make this decision. Child porters should not be employed.*

—Dr. Jim Duff, MD is the founder and Director of the International Porter Protection Group (IPPG), www.ippg.net ; IPPG has initiated projects for the benefit of porters' health and safety worldwide, including porter shelters, clothing banks, and rescue posts)

Times are changing for the better with groups like International Porter Protection Group (www.ippg.net), Porters Progress U.K. (www.portersprogress.org), Community Action Nepal (www.canepal.org.uk), International Mountain Explorers Club (www.mountainexplorers.org), and KEEP (www.keepnepal.org) raising awareness and setting up clothing banks, shelters, aid posts and other programs and resources for porters.

Porters are at the low end of a hierarchical society. In Nepalese terms, people in this position rarely complain, even at times when physical harm may be occurring. Thus, as the employer, either directly or through an agency, maintain a watch on the safety of your porters along the way to help ensure that the pattern of neglect and exploitation does not continue. That said, properly engaging a porter and guide is encouraged, if you are so inclined, and can greatly enhance your experience while providing a valuable source of income. In fact, if you travel without a porter or guide, then you might be missing an extraordinary opportunity to get closer to the heart and soul of Nepali culture.

PORTER POETRY

Poem

Even though my soul has been torn, here I am laughing.
Even though my very being is in fragments, I have somehow survived.
As long as there is one drop of blood in my body,
Until life's last instant, I will always foster this love.
When I die I will be thinking of it – my education.
But now it is just a dream that cannot become reality.
If I was a flower, I would bloom, but I cannot for all of the thorns.
If my love was for anything else I could forget it.
I cannot forget my desire to learn, and the road is covered in thorns.
How can I laugh with my heart so filled with a love for learning?
How can I laugh?
--Santaki B.K. (translation by Ben Ayers)

Assets

Today, a Nepali's morality
Only considers possessions.

Respected porters, brothers –
Today, a Nepali's identity
Has become selfish.

Respected porters, brothers –
We're only here as long as our physical health is.
Of course, we will become wealthy and happy.

Respected porters, brothers –
If your soul is content and peaceful
Your creativity can build a Taj Mahal!

Respected porters, brothers –
Make your hardship into a possession.
Soak this earth with your sweat.
Make a storehouse for your sweat.
-- Nanda Raj Rai (translated by Ben Ayers)

FEMALE CREW AND GENDER DISCRIMINATION

Nowadays, women as well as men are available as porters and guides. In order to eliminate the potential of harassment, female travelers and families with children might be especially interested in hiring female crew.

It is unfortunate that in certain countries, women are often relegated to a lower status. In much of Asia, females face disadvantages in school enrollment, control over household income and work burden, employment and earnings disparities and representation in government and policy making. Some women, particularly in western Nepal, are kicked out of the household during monthly menses and forced to live in a shed to face hypothermia, hunger, insect and animal bites and more.

The gender bias is ominously reflected in the birth ratio statistics of Nepal's mighty neighbors, **China** and **India**. Birth rates in these nascent economic giants favor males over females by a ratio of more than 1.1. That is, out of every 110 males born, there are less than 100 females born. **'Gendercide'**, in other words, excess female mortality, including **missing girls at birth** (sex-selective abortions, infanticide, and neglect), was projected in **2008** to be **3.9 million women worldwide**. China and India accounted for **more than 50%** of the estimated deaths.

Sadly, in **Nepal** between 10,000 to 15,000 women and girls are betrayed by their own families and sold for labor and even to the flesh trade in India (and an additional 7,500 children are trafficked internally). **Anuradha Koirala** co-founded **Maiti Nepal** (www.maitinepal.org), an organization that offers refuge centers in Kathmandu and along the Indo-Nepal border for women rescued from Indian brothels. She received the **Hero of the Year 2010** from media giant CNN for her role in combatting sex-slavery and helping victims of human trafficking. Maiti Nepal aims not only to end abduction for the flesh trade and child prostitution but aspires to eliminate all forms of domestic abuse and exploitation (the Nepal Youth Foundation is another such organization with laudable aims, http://nepalyouthfoundation.org.

The wide gender gap is unmistakable in **Nepal's literacy rates**, with some **differences between males and females greater than 30% in rural areas and 25% in urban areas**. Although a 2008–09 study of eight of Nepal's districts found the maternal mortality rate had been halved since 1991, there has been a disturbing rise in the suicide rate of women of reproductive age, making **suicide the leading cause of death** in the surveyed districts.

Women who are able to find employment as porters and guides will have economic and other opportunities that are unheard of for traditional Nepali women who live relatively sheltered existences determined by oppressive, patriarchal rules. Empowering Women of Nepal is a Pokhara organization run by Three Sisters Adventure Trekking that is training and promoting female guides, and Nepali Healing Home (formerly known as, The Nepali Yoga Women Trust) also based in Pokhara, aims at helping women improve their socio-economic situation. Venus Treks (www.venustreks.com) offers touring and trekking services with female guides and staff for female travelers.

MAPS

Maps are an integral tool for travel in Nepal and provide vital route information, terrain characteristics and perspective. Especially important are features of elevation and settlement locations. Nepal-produced, elaborate maps are available at bookstores in Nepal, especially in Thamel, Kathmandu, and Lakeside, Pokhara. Trails, villages, and contour lines are shown on most of them although not always accurately; many maps in Nepal have been drawn by people who have not traveled in the featured region.

Maps of Nepal are also available at online stores, such as www.mapsworldwide.com, www.stanfords.co.uk, www.cordee.co.uk, www.omnimap.com, www.amazon.co.uk, www.pilgrimsonlineshop.com and www. amazon.com.

ACCOMMODATIONS

Summary: Tourists in Kathmandu and Pokhara can choose from the full range of accommodations and services, from bare minimum to five-star. Out on the trails, travelers have a variety of choices from camping with a retinue of porters, cooks and guides to camping on one's own at the 'billion star hotel' (ie, skies full of stars blinking above the enchanting landscape). Otherwise, select from simple lodges to well-furnished hotels, or try home stay with local residents for a unique experience. Nepal travel has accommodations and possibilities for every tourist.

Depending on your style there is something available for every budget in Nepal. The main tourist centers of Kathmandu, Pokhara and Chitwan have everything up to first class accommodation during your visit.

In Kathmandu, the majority of tourists stay in an area named Thamel. This globetrotter ghetto may seem like neon-Nirvana to some travelers, whereas to others it is sensory overload. The area has an overabundance of facilities and profusion of signs promoting hotels, restaurants, bars, bakeries, spas and more. Despite the seeming chaos, Thamel is a suitable place for arranging travel logistics and picking up gear. The growing influx of Chinese tourists prefer the southeastern corner of Thamel, now referred to as Chinatown. Other laid-back areas of Kathmandu that are popular with tourists include Paknajol to the immediate northwest of Thamel and an area referred to as Freak Street near Kathmandu's Durbar Square. Additionally, the area around Baudhnath Stupa has numerous lodges. These locations have many facilities that cater to tourists. Several upper-end hotels are found along Durbar Marg, the road leading to the front gate of the former palace as well as in the Lazimpat area of Kathmandu and the neighboring city of Patan.

Nepal's popular trekking routes offer a wide range of accommodation, typically surrounded by majestic natural scenery. Away from the tourist highways, foreigners in rural areas are few and far between and if not camping or staying in simple lodges, then home stay accommodation will have to be arranged, a recommended option in this welcoming country for getting to know your hosts and more of Nepal's cultural treasures!

In fact, home stay can be the most memorable way of traveling and will likely turn into the highlight of your travels. It will offer an insider's view of the culture and daily routine of the people. The lifestyle in the rural hills is typically untouched by modern amenities.

Always be sure to remove footwear before entering a home. Visitors will likely be shown where to sit and offered a drink of tea. Do your best to eat when and what the family eats or offers food to you. You will probably be asked many questions by your eager hosts. A private room might be offered for sleeping or you will end up on a carpet on the floor. Relax and enjoy! Ask whether the family has a toilet facility or if there is a shared one for the community. In much of Nepal, there are no private latrines whatsoever, and you will have to use the great outdoors. Find a sheltered spot away from running water and bury the excreta at least 6 inches (15 cm), or at least cover it with stones. If you use paper, then carry a lighter or matches and burn any used toilet paper at once.

Respect local customs and follow the lead of your hosts. Do not show affection, hand-holding by the opposite sexes and kissing in public is unthinkable to most Nepalis. After all is said and done, if your intentions are in the right place, then actions will follow. Errors, might they be made, will be easily overlooked if you are doing your best. When departing, the amount of payment for home stay will often be up to you.

Those with gear can camp along the way. Tents and stoves will certainly attract a crowd in places that have rarely seen camping equipment. National parks and conservation areas will have designated fee sites. Organized treks will arrange these by the agency. On your own, look near villages for campsites on terraces that have already been harvested and clearings in the forest.

If staying in lodges, pay the standard fees. In the end, remember that accommodation during your visit will be a good bargain while you explore the magnificent spectacle of the Himalaya!

COMMUNICATIONS, INTERNET, PHONE AND POST

Summary: Nepal is fast becoming as wired and tuned-in as the rest of the world, although advances and services are less noticeable outside main urban centers. Nevertheless, it is now possible to connect with friends, colleagues and family back home from some of the highest and most remote locations on the planet.

Nepal is advancing in all technology sectors, and even in rural regions, service is becoming available but still mobile coverage can be spotty and internet connections slow. The following information will help you to stay in touch with friends and loved ones during your Himalayan travels:

Communications to and from Nepal. Nepal's international country telephone code is 977, with city codes of 01 for Kathmandu and 061 for Pokhara (you might have to eliminate the zero depending on from where you are calling). When calling home, keep in mind that Nepal is five-and-three-quarters hours ahead of Greenwich Mean Time (**GMT**) and Coordinated Universal Time (**UCT**). Wi-fi and Internet cafes abound in Kathmandu and Pokhara for sending and receiving electronic mail.

Mobile Phone Communications. Mobile phones in Nepal use a Subscriber Identity Module (SIM) card. The SIM card is basically a memory chip inserted into a phone and can be transferred between phones. SIM cards may be purchased at the sales offices of service providers, NTC and NCELL are the two largest that offer nationwide service. Purchasing a SIM requires an original passport as well as a photocopy of both the passport and visa for Nepal. SIM cards are now available at the international airport arrival terminal. The Global System for Mobile Communication (GSM) network and the Code Division Multiple Access (CDMA) network are both in operation in Nepal. The best coverage for remote areas may be the CDMA network.

Internet Communications. Wi-fi connections are now widely available in most tourist areas in urban areas in restaurants and hotels and it is making it up to the trekking routes, too. Internet access is also available for laptops from mobile phone service providers via pen drive-sized data card devices. The devices operate through a USB port and fees generally depend on MB of usage. Additionally, internet cafes abound in Kathmandu and Pokhara for sending and receiving electronic mail. Occasionally, internet shops are encountered along trekking routes, although connections in remote places can be slow and unreliable.

Post Office Kathmandu's main post office is in Sundhara, to the west and across the road from Tundikhel Parade Ground near Bhimsen Tower (also known as *Dharahara*). Hours are 10 AM–4 PM, closed Saturday. For receiving incoming mail, you might try the following general address (keep in mind that an import duty will likely be assessed and there are occasional reports of loss):

Post Restante, Kathmandu General Post Office, Kathmandu, Nepal

Postage rates from Nepal are calculated according to the following regions: **1)** SAARC countries (Afghanistan, Bangladesh, Bhutan, India, the Maldives, Pakistan, and Sri Lanka), **2)** Asia (not including SAARC countries, South Korea and Japan), **3)** Europe, South Korea and Japan, **4)** the Americas, Australia and New Zealand. As of February 2012, Postcard and letter (up to .7 ounces or 20 grams) rates by region are respectively the following:

1) 15 NRS/18 NRS, **2)** 22 NRS/30 NRS, **3)** 25 NRS/35 NRS, **4)** 30 NRS/40 NRS

PHOTOGRAPHY AND VIDEO

Summary: Nepal is a land of vibrant contrasts, robust scenery and wide-ranging diversity in culture and geography. Simply put, Nepal is a photographer's paradise. From lush jungles, to ancient villages surrounded by terraced fields to the highest peaks on the planet, you will

have much to capture for memory's sake and to show family and friends back home and within your social networks.

Nepal's captivating scenery and people will provide much inspiration for photography and filming whether you are a beginner or an expert. The lowland jungles are lush and home to exotic plant and animal wildlife. The farmland of the terraced hills provides a rich bounty of nature's splendor and timeless way of life, and the bustling cities are filled with temples and monuments at nearly every corner. Finally, the highest peaks on earth are one of the world's greatest spectacles. Wherever you go in Nepal, and however your travel style, you will want to capture the blend of images that you encounter.

Most travelers make do with a digital camera or video recorder. You will want to bring spare batteries and memory cards. Recharging batteries is possible even in remote areas but requires the correct apparatus, including a universal adapter (Nepal's electricity run 200 volts/50 cycle). When recharging is not possible, then you will need extra batteries. You do not want the feeling of looking at an astonishing view and experiencing a festival scene without the means to capture it! Spare memory cards are a must, too, especially on long treks, as Nepal will provide you with many opportunities to put them to use.

More experienced and serious photographers might want to bring a chest pack and carry extra lenses and perhaps a polarizing or graduated filter and a tripod. In the highlands, battery life can be prolonged by keeping the battery warm, perhaps in a pocket where it can pick up body heat and consider storing batteries inside your sleeping bag at night while sleeping.

The natural light of Nepal's surroundings is best around sunrise and sunset for photography. Beginners might also want to remember to bring along the camera's instruction manual for maximizing capabilities and taking home the best shots.

Please keep in mind that while traveling, the people you encounter might not want to be photographed. Although most people in Nepal are quite friendly and welcoming and do not mind being a part of your photographic collection, there will be exceptions. Please respect that it is a personal choice and not all people want their picture taken or their children's, especially if they are not feeling at their best, are in work clothes or doing something considered private. Be sure to ask before photographing and filming people and while visiting inside monasteries and temples, too. Most of the time it is completely accepted but when it is not, the wish needs to be respected.

Often having a conversation with a person and describing what it is that you find beautiful or interesting and want to photograph can ease tensions if there is initial reluctance. Sometimes you will be asked to send prints to the local people whom you photographed. Unless you intend to do so, then it is best not to make any promises. Today's digital camera also allows you to show images immediately after snapping them. If you plan to send photos, then write down an accurate address, and often trekkers coming in after you and your trekking agency can assist with delivery.

Nepal will be a great chance to put your camera and video recorder to use with sensational landscapes and cultural attractions. You will relish the memories that images provide and sharing them on a social networks will make it all the more enjoyable.

BEFORE VISITNG NEPAL AND WHAT TO BRING

Summary: Most of Nepal's tourists come for trekking in the Himalaya, an unforgettable experience of a lifetime. Nepal is also renowned for jungle safaris, rafting, paragliding, mountain biking, and other adventure sports and leisure activities. If you arrive prepared for your chosen activities in one of the most scenic and exciting countries on earth, then your journey will be all the more successful and satisfying.

Note: Nepal Immigration has updated its procedures. Please post your application online for a visa up to two weeks before your arrival (http://www.online.nepalimmigration.gov.np/tourist-visa).

Before you visit Nepal and the Himalaya, it is best to have the necessary vaccinations although serious illness in travelers is rare. Vaccination recommendations are found in the *Health is Himalayan Wealth* section. Plan a few months ahead of time to obtain the full immunization course. Secondly, arrive with at least two passport size photos and cash for the visa on demand at the airport and border crossings and more photos will be needed for trekking permits and TIMS cards in Nepal. Finally, you will want to pack sufficient gear and keep in mind that many items can be purchased or rented in Nepal but often authenticity and durability is questionable. Essential items, for example, hiking footwear, should be brought from home. The gear you need to bring will depend on your activities and the season as well.

Many special-interest activities are possible these days with themes of art, flora and fauna, health, meditation, natural history, religion, team building, education, yoga and more. Adventure sports include rock climbing, mountain biking, rafting, kayaking, canyoning, paragliding (and parahawking), bunjee jumping, and more.

Trekking is Nepal's most popular tourist activity and is essentially hiking extended routes that generally have facilities along the way for room and board. During a trek, travelers spend nights in well-furnished hotels, simple lodges, camp, or stay in the homes of local people. Depending on your trekking style and goals, you will want to consider bringing the following with you to Nepal:

• **base layer of clothing**, long underwear of polypropylene, nylon, wool, or silk
• **quick-drying outer wear**
• **camera** and photographic equipment including **extra batteries** and **memory cards**
• **earplugs**, more than one pair (homes and lodges often have thin walls, vehicles have blaring stereos, and dogs howl late at night)
• **elastic bands, nylon line** (parachute cord): for lashings, hanging laundry, makeshift shoestrings)
• **feminine hygiene materials**: women might consider bringing an ecological, reusable **menstrual cup** (*eg*, **Mooncup**) that collects fluids, as an alternative to carrying disposable tampons or other materials
• **lightweight sandals**, foam/rubber footwear: for use after the day's hike is over, around the room, lodge, and village; especially useful in toilet and shower areas
• **footwear that supports the ankles** and that you have tried and gotten used to wearing
• **gloves**
• **handkerchief** or bandanna (more than one) , used as face mask for cold and dust, or to dry cups, plates, hands and more
• **hat with brim**, and **warm hat** that covers the ears
• **headlamp (flashlight)**
• **high-energy snacks**
• **insect repellent**, including essential oils of eucalyptus or citronella
• **makeshift shelter**: emergency blanket (aluminized polyester)/plastic sheeting/bivouac shelter
• **pack** that you have tried and gotten used to
• **backpack cover** ones made in Kathmandu are a good value

- **plastic bags**, especially useful for keeping gear dry in wet weather and general organization
- **personal first-aid kit** (see Health is Himalayan Wealth section for recommendations)
- **pocket knife**
- **portable music player**
- **rain poncho** -- cape large enough to cover self and pack
- **reading materials**—books/magazine/electronic files
- **rechargeable batteries, charger, and universal adapter**
- **skirts, mid-calf to above the ankle for women**
- **sleeping bag**
- **sleeping bag liner** or sheet for use between a lodge's unwashed sheets/blankets
- **socks**, several pairs
- **spare eyeglasses or contact lenses**
- **sunglasses** (**UV-protective**; be aware that inexpensive sunglasses might do more harm than good by shading the eyes and dilating pupils which allows more UV exposure)
- **sunscreen and lip balm**, ayurvedic sunblock cream is available in Kathmandu
- **sweater** (aka, jumper)
- **toiletries**, including **biodegradable soap** (ayurvedic soap is available in Nepal)
- **umbrella** both to protect against sunlight in warm sunny lowlands and in the monsoon
- **universal adapter** for recharging batteries/electronic devices
- **water bottle**; at least 32-ounce (1-liter) capacity per person
- **water-purification materials**
- **windproof jacket**

Nepal's trails are steep and every addition to your load counts! Review your personal gear list, and eliminate non-essentials before you depart your home country. Decent, second-hand camping and mountaineering equipment used by other trekkers and climbers on Himalayan expeditions is often available for sale or rent in Kathmandu, Pokhara, and Namche Bazaar (Everest Region).

If you play a portable musical instrument, consider bringing it along. A harmonica, flute et cetera can quickly ease communication barriers. Consider other social and entertainment skills that you might share, for example, portrait drawing and simple card and magic tricks.

Make copies of your itinerary and important documents and leave them with a friend or family member back home and copy to your email or electronic devices before you visit Nepal to ease your mind for appreciating all Nepal has to offer. And most of all be prepared to be flexible!

"All things are ready, if our mind be so." -William Shakespeare

MORE ON GEAR AND ESSENTIALS

Summary: Nepal has some of the most glorious scenery and panoramas on the planet. Despite the natural splendor and welcoming people, geographical extremes and remote, challenging locations can be inhospitable to human existence. Bringing the right clothing and gear is essential. Take care of your equipment and it will take care of you allowing more freedom to explore Nepal's beauty and treasures.

Nepal is home to jungle lowlands up to the highest mountains on earth. The terrain and geography require that you be outfitted for extremes. If you have the right gear and clothing, then it will take care of you on your journeys. Being properly equipped will allow the ability and comfort to make the most of Himalayan encounters from the southern plains to frosty peaks.

First of all, it is recommended to have proper footwear that has been personally tested and is comfortable. The hills and high mountain trails and jungle paths can be punishing to footwear. Find something durable that supports the ankles. Your feet and legs will be doing a lot of work in this challenging terrain and you will want to take care of them as best as possible.

Next in importance in gear and essentials is a quality pack. Many well-designed packs are available these days. Choose one that feels comfortable when full, allows easy access and can expand volume as needed. Equipment and supplies that porters carry can be packed in sturdy, bright-colored (for recognition) duffel bags, and bring a small lock to secure zippers.

Bring suitable and sufficient clothing. Hiking through Nepal's rural terrain can cause a swift buildup of body heat, especially carrying a loaded pack up a steep incline. In high altitude areas, the temperature will drop rapidly, especially at sundown, in the shade and if clothes are wet and cold from sweat. It is important to have the ability to remove or add items to adjust quickly to conditions.

A first layer of clothing should keep you dry by wicking moisture away from the skin to the next layer. Thermals made with polypropylene, can be a good inner layer. Nylon is durable. Silk is lightweight but needs extra care and might easily come apart at the seams. The next layer should provide warmth. Wool is traditionally chosen for the cold because it stays warm when wet. A sweater or synthetic fiber-insulated fleece (pile) jacket works well in wet weather and also dries quickly. The outer layer should add warmth and keep you dry as well. A waterproof, breathable shell is recommended.

A down or synthetic-fiber sleeping bag is usually necessary for comfort at temperatures below freezing. Many lodges have blankets, but you cannot always depend on them, especially during busy times and they are not regularly washed. Trekkers along the popular routes manage without a sleeping bag, but going without one is not advised on high-altitude routes. In lodges along popular trekking trails, mattresses and pillows are available, but not everywhere, especially during high season and when away from the main pathways. You will want to bring your own portable mattress if planning to get away from the main routes and camp.

Bring a pair of sunglasses that absorb ultraviolet light. A visor to shade the eyes from the sun is an ideal addition. Umbrellas can be used not only against rainfall but to protect against the sunlight on bright, hot days. Consider taking collapsible ski poles or Nepali made walking sticks to ease the load and impact on the knees.

Each traveler should have a water container of at least 1-quart (liter) capacity. Plastic and lightweight stainless-steel or aluminum containers can be found in trekking shops in Nepal. Bring a headlamp or small flashlight (torch) and spare batteries, especially to power the modern camera. Consider earplugs (several pairs, as they are easily lost) for noisy hotels and vehicle transport.

Visitors traveling in the lowlands during the warmer months or during the monsoon might want to have insect repellent and a mosquito net while sleeping.

Second-hand gear and essentials used by other trekkers and climbers on Himalayan expeditions is often available for sale or rent in Kathmandu, Pokhara, and remote hubs like Namche Bazaar in the Khumbu. Some trekkers sell equipment by way of notice boards in restaurants, hotels, and at the Kathmandu Environmental Education Project which also has a gear cache for porters.

Locally manufactured gear often has a fake designer label. It might only last one trek if that, but some is more durable. There are now genuine outlet stores in Thamel and along Durbar Marg, the road that leads from the former royal palace turned into Narayanhiti National Museum (and in Namche Bazaar). Sherpa Adventure Gear brand has showrooms in both Kathmandu (near Jai Nepal Cinema Hall) and Pokhara (Lakeside at Barahi Chowk). Some people are able to pick up everything they need in Kathmandu or Pokhara, but it is safer to arrive at least minimally prepared.

Most trekkers carry reading and writing materials. A pack of cards or miniature versions of popular board games (such as Scrabble) can be a good way to pass time at a restaurant as well as to get to know fellow travelers. Find room to bring portable games in your pack along with the essentials keeping in mind, Nepal's trails are steep and your backpack load weight counts! Review your gear list, and pare down non-essentials beforehand.

NEPALI LANGUAGE

Nepal has over 90 distinct languages. Nepali is the national language and used as the second tongue by about half of the population. Nepali is an Indo-European language derived from Sanskrit and became one of India's official languages in 1992. It is written in Devanagari script (as are Hindi and Sanskrit), and there are several sounds in Nepali that are not common in English and transliteration will not be precise. There are many variations in how it is spoken, and efforts to speak Nepali will set you apart and be appreciated by your hosts!

GLOSSARY

Transliteration of the Nepali as well as the actual Devanagari script is provided to facilitate understanding. If pronunciation proves difficult, show the script with the Nepali word or phrase in Devanagari to the person with whom you are communicating.

Transliteration pronunciation guidelines:
a as the *a* in about or the *u* in cup, hut (**å** is nasalization of the **a** sound)
aa as the *a* in far or *o* in top, dot (**åå** is nasalization of the **aa** sound)
e as the *e* in latte or *ey* in whey or the *ay* in day
i as the *i* in miss, tip, hit

o as the *o* in more, grow, snow, crow
u as the *ue* in true or *oo* in roof, moo (**ů** is nasalization of the **u** sound)

   D, **T** and **N** (capitalized letters): curl the tongue back so that the tip of it touches the roof of the mouth while producing the sound. Otherwise, the lower case **d**, **t** and **n** sounds are made with the tip of the tongue toward the front teeth

   The letter **h** after a consonant indicates aspiration or a breathing out with the accompanying sound with the exception of *ch*, which is not aspirated (breath is not expelled with the sound) while *chh*, is aspirated.

FAMILY

ENGLISH	TRANSLITERATION	DEVANAGARI
mother	aamaa	आमा
father	buwaa, baabu	बुवा or बाबु
older sister	didi	दिदी
younger sister	bahini	बहिनी
older brother	daai, daaju	दाइ or दाजु
younger brother	bhaai	भाइ
daughter	chori	छोरी
son	choraa	छोरा
you (familiar)	timi	तिमी
you (formal)	tapaai	तपाई
she/he (familiar)	u	उ
she/he (formal)	wahåå	वहाँ

113

I	ma	म
me	malaai	मलाई
my	mero	मेरो

FOOD AND DRINK

ENGLISH	TRANSLITERATION	DEVANAGARI
appetizing, delicious, tasty	miTho or swaadishT	मीठो, स्वादिष्ट
apple	syaau	स्याउ
banana	keraa	केरा
basil	tulsi	तुल्सी
black tea	kaalo chiyaa	कालोचिया
chickpeas (garbanzo beans)	chanaa	चना
chutney (pickled salsa)	achaar	अचार
coriander	dhaniyåå	धनियाँ
diarrhea	pakhaalaa, disaa	पखाला or दिसा
distilled, local alcoholic drink	raksi	रक्सी
egg	ful, aNDaa	फुलor अण्डा
enough	pugyo, bhayo	पुग्यो orभयो
fermented, locally made alcoholic beverage	jååD, chhyaang	जाँड or छ्याङ्

fermented millet alcoholic beverage	tongbaa, tumbaa	तोङ्बा or तुम्बा
flatbread (unleavened bread)	roTi , chapaati	रोटी or चपाती
food/meal (rice, lentils vegetables, ie, daal-bhaat-tarakaari)	khaanaa	खाना
ginger	aduwaa	अदुवा
green leafy vegetables (e.g., spinach, mustard greens)	saag	साग
lemon	kaagati	कागती
lentils	daal	दाल
less sugar	chini kam	चिनीकम
maize (corn)	makai	मकै
meat, flesh, muscles	maasu	मासु
milk	dudh	दूध
mixed vegetable dish	tarakaari or sabji	तरकारी or सब्जी
potato	aalu	आलु
monosodium glutamate (MSG)	ajinomoTo	अजीनोमोटो
rice (cooked)	bhaat	भात

salt	nun	नून
salty	nunilo	नुनिलो
sour	amilo	अमिलो
soybeans	bhaTmaas	भटमास
spicy	piro	पिरो
sugar	chini	चिनी
sweet	guliyo	गुलियो
sweet milk tea	chiyaa (or, more precisely, dudhko chiyaa	चिया (दूधकोचिया)
to boil	umaalnu, usinnu	उमाल्नु or उसिन्नु
to cook	pakaaunu	पकाउनु
to eat	khaanu	खानु
to heat up/make warm	tataaunu	तताउनु
water	paani	पानी
yogurt (aka, curd)	dahi	दही

ADDITIONAL VOCABULARY

ENGLISH	TRANSLITERATION	DEVANAGARI
animal	janaawar	जनावर
bag	jholaa	झोला
big	Thulo	ठूलो
bird	charaa	चरा

blanket	sirak, kammal, kambal	सिरकor कम्मल or कम्बल
bridge	pul	पुल
Buddhist monastery	gombaa, gumbaa	गोम्बा orगुम्बा
Buddhist scroll painting	thaankaa	थान्का
Buddhist structure/memorial	stupaa, chorTen	स्तुपाorचोर्टेन
butterfly	putali	पुतली
cheap	sasto	सस्तो
cicada	jhaaukiri	झाउकिरी
clean	safaa	सफा
cold (adj)	chiso	चिसो
cold (weather)	jaaDo	जाडो
correct, good	Thik , raamro	ठीक or राम्रो
danger	khataraa	खतरा
diarrhea	pakhaalaa,disaa	पखाला or दिसा
dirty	fohor	फोहोर
donation	daan	दान
down (adv)	tala	तल
evening, dusk	belukaa, sååjha	बेलुका or साँझ
expensive	mahågo	महँगो
flower	phul	फूल
forest	ban, juNgal	बनor जङ्गल

gateway, village archway	kaaNi	काणी
hat or cap made of cloth fabric	Topi	टोपी
help, assistance	maddat	मद्दत
here	yahåå	यहाँ
hills	pahaaD	पहाड
Himalayan range	himaalaya	हिमालय
Hindu temple	mandir	मन्दिर
hour	ghanTaa	घन्टा
injured	ghaaite	घाइते
kerosene	maTTitel	मट्टितेल
key	chaabi	चाबी
lake	taal	ताल
landslip	pahiro	पहिरो
leech	jukaa	जुका
left (direction)	baayåå	बायाँ
long	laamo	लामो
love	maayaa, prem	मायाor प्रेम
lowland plains	tarai	तराई
map	naksaa	नक्सा
maybe	holaa	होला
medicinal herbs	jaDibuTi	जडीबूटी

money	paisaa, rupaiyåå	पैसा or रुपैयाँ
monkey	båådar	बाँदर
morning	bihaana	बिहान
Mount Everest	sagarmaathaa	सगरमाथा
mountains, range	himaal, parbat	हिमाल or पर्वत
new	nayåå	नयाँ
night	raat	रात
no, is not	hoina , åha, chhaina	होइन or अँह or छैन
not good	naraamro	नराम्रो
oil, can also mean fuel, gasoline	tel	तेल
old	puraano	पुरानो
orphan	anaatha	अनाथ
party	bhoj	भोज
fast, quick	chhiTo	छिटो
prayer inscribed stone or wall of such prayer stones (also means 'jewel')	maaNe	माणी
rain	paani parnu	पानी पर्नु
ready, prepared	tayaar	तयार
religion, religious practice, duty	dharma	धर्म

rest area, usually with a platform and shade tree	chautaaraa	चौतारा
rhododendron (red rhododendron)	guråås (laaliguråås)	गुराँस (लालीगुराँस)
ridge	DååDaa	डाँडा
right (direction)	daayåå	दायाँ
river	nadi, kholaa	नदी or खोला
room	koTaa	कोठा
room for sleeping	sutne koTaa	सुत्नेकोठा
route, path, trail, road	baaTo	बाटो
service	sewaa	सेवा
shepards' shelter	goTh	गोठ
short	chhoTo	छोटो
sick, ill	biraami	बिरामी
slow	Dhilo	ढिलो
small	saano	सानो
snow	hiů	हिउँ
shop (n.)	pasal	पसल
straight	sidhaa	सीधा
strike (closure)	banda	बन्द
suffering, hardship	du-kha	दुःख
sunlight	ghaam	घाम

tall, high	aglo	अग्लो
thanks	dhanyabaad	धन्यबाद
that	tyo	त्यो
there	tyahåå	त्यहाँ
this	yo	यो
to be tired	thakaai laagnu	थकाइलाग्नु
to do	garnu	गर्नु
to go	jaanu	जानु
to walk	hiDnu	हिंड्नु
today	aaja	आज
toilet	charpi	चर्पी
tomorrow	bholi	भोलि
tree	rukh	रूख
up (adv)	maathi	माथि
very, much	ekdam, dherai	एकदम , धेरै
village	gaaů	गाउँ
vipassana	vipashyanaa	विपश्यना
walking stick	lauro	लौरो
What?	ke	के?
When?	kahile	कहिले ?
Where?	kataa, kahåå	कता or कहाँ ?
Which?	kun	कुन ?

Who?	ko ho	को हो ?
Why?	kina	किन ?
worship/prayer/ritual	pujaa	पूजा
yes, is	ho, hunchha, hajur (polite form)	हो or हुन्छ or हजुर
yesterday	hijo	हिजो

USEFUL WORDS AND PHRASES

ENGLISH	TRANSLITERATION	DEVANAGARI
Hello (and goodbye)	namaste (or, more formally, namaskaar)	नमस्ते (or नमस्कार)
How are you?	tapaailaai kasto chha?	तपाईलाई कस्तो छ?
What is (happening/going on)?	ke chha?	केछ ?
See you again (goodbye)!	pheri bheTaulaa	फेरी भेटौला
How much?	kati ho, kati parchha	कतिहो or कति पर्छ?

Thank you	dhanyabaad	धन्यवाद
I am sorry/I beg your pardon	malaai maaph garnus	मलाई माफ गर्नुस्
I have diarrhea	malaai pakhaalaa (or disaa) laageko chha	मलाई पखाला(दिसा) लागेको छ
I have a fever	malaai jwaro aayeko chha	मलाई ज्वरो आएको छ
This tastes good!	yo miTho chha	यो मिठो छ
I am thirsty	malaai pyaas (or, tirkhaa) laageko chha	मलाई प्यास(तिर्खा) लागेको छ
I am hungry	malaai bhok laageko chha	मलाई भोक लागेको छ
Is there a shop here?	yahåå pasal chha holaa?	यहाँ पसल छ होला ?
Please don't add tasty powder (MSG/ajinomoto)	kripyaa khaanaamaa ajinomoTo naraakhnu holaa	कृपया खानामा अजिनोमोटो नराख्नुहोला
I am a vegetarian	ma shaakaahaari hů	म शाकाहारी हुँ
I do not eat meat	ma maasu nakhaane	म मासु नखाने
Is food available here?	yahåå khaanaa paainchha?	यहाँ खाना पाइन्छ ?
May I stay at your house?	ma tapaaiko gharmaa basna sakchhu?	म तपाईंको घरमा बस्न सक्छु ?
Where can I stay?	ma kahåå basna sakchhu holaa?	म कहाँ बस्न सक्छु होला ?
Is there a place to stay here?	yahåå basne suvidhaa chha holaa	यहाँ बस्ने सुविधा छ होला ?

123

Is there a lodge here?	yahåå laj chha holaa? (or, yahåå sutna paaincha holaa)	यहाँ लज छ होला ?(यहाँ सुत्न पाइन्छ होला ?)
What is the name of thisvillage?	yo gaaůko naam ke ho?	या गाउँको नाम के हो ?
What time is it?	ahile kati bajyo? (or, samaya kati bhayo holaa?)	अहिले कति बज्यो ?(समय कति भयोहोला?)
I don't know	malaai thaahaa chhaina	मलाई थाहा छैन
How much is it?	yo kati ho? (or, yasko kati ho?)	यो कति हो ? (यसको कति हो ?)
How many?	kati waTaa? (or, kati?)	कतिवटा ? (कति ?)
Do you have children?	tapaaikaa bacchaa (chhoraa chhori) chhan?	तपाईंका बच्चा (छोराछोरी) छन् ?
Are you married?	tapaaiko bibaaha bhayo?	तपाईंको विवाह भयो ?
How old are you?	tapaaiko umer kati bhayo?	तपाईंको उमेर कति भयो ?
Have you eaten?	tapaaile khaanaakhaanu bhayo?	तपाईंले खाना खानुभयो ?
I have eaten	maile khaaisake	मैले खाइसकें
Where are you going?	tapaai kahåå jåådai hunuhunchha?	तपाई कहाँ जाँदै हुनुहुन्छ ?
I am going to…	ma ….. Thaaůmaa jåådai chhu	म .... ठाउँमा जाँदैछु

What is this?	yo ke ho?	यो के हो ?
Where are you from?	tapaai kahåå baaTa aaunu bhayeko ho?	तपाईं कहाँबाट आउनुभएको हो ?
I am from...	ma ..... baaTa aayeko hů	म .... बाट आएको हूँ
Which country?	kun desh?	कुन देश ?
What is your name?	tapaaiko naam ke ho?	तपाईंको नाम के हो?
My name is	mero naam ... ho	मेरो नाम ... हो
I am fine	malaai Thik chha (or, ma sanchai chhu)	मलाई ठिक छ (म सञ्चै छु)
How are you?	tapaailaai kasto chha?(or, tapaailaai sanchai chha?)	तपाईंलाई कस्तो छ?(तपाईंलाई सञ्चै छ ?)
I like	malaai manparchha	मलाई मनपर्छ
I do not like?	malaai manpardaina	मलाईमनपर्दैन

NUMERALS

ROMAN NUMERAL	NEPALI NUMERAL	TRANSLITERATION	DEVANAGARI
0	०	shunya	शून्य
1	१	ek	एक
2	२	dui	दुई
3	३	tin	तीन
4	४	chaar	चार
5	५	pååch	पाँच
6	६	chha	छ
7	७	saat	सात
8	८	aaTh	आठ
9	९	nau	नौ
10	१०	das	दस
20	२०	bis	बीस
30	३०	tis	तीस
40	४०	chaalis	चालीस
50	५०	pachaas	पचास
60	६०	saaThi	साठी
70	७०	sattari	सत्तरी
80	८०	asi	असी
90	९०	nabbe	नब्बे
100	१००	say, ek say	सयor एकसय
500	५००	pååch say	पाँचसय
1000	१०००	hajaar, ek hajaar	हजार or एकहजार

TIPS FOR TRAVELING NEPAL

Summary: Nepal's treks, safaris, city tours of World Heritage splendour, adventure sports and leisure activities offer an exhilarating range of holiday options. With a varied landscape from jungle plains to the highest peaks on the planet, Nepal has a wide selection of topography and eco-diversity with many natural and cultural treasures. The following are a few tips to make the most of your journey to this Himalayan nation.

First of all, Scan a copy of your passport into your email account and make hard photocopies of your passport, itinerary and important documents and leave them with friends or family back home and keep a set for yourself, too.

Tips for Traveling Safely in Nepal:

Medical Insurance. Does your coverage apply overseas and include rescue insurance or will you need to get supplemental coverage?

Register with you embassy on arrival along with your itinerary. They can help find and notify you if needed for emergency purposes or to notify your friends and family should the need arise for you.

Let your credit card company know that you will be traveling and keep their phone numbers handy.

Meet with your physician several months prior to departure and check that you have the necessary vaccinations.

Trekking Tips for Nepal:

Nepal's trekking trails are steep and every addition to the weight of your travel pack counts! Review your gear and clothing list, and pare down items beforehand.

Bring easily donned and doffed clothing layers. Hiking Nepal's steep terrain can cause a swift build-up of body heat, especially carrying a loaded pack up a sun-drenched hill. In high altitude areas, the temperature will drop rapidly, especially in the shaded areas of the mighty Himalaya, when the sun has set or is behind the clouds, and more so if your clothes are wet and cold from sweat. It is important to have the ability to remove or add items to adjust quickly to conditions.

Bring a bright-color duffel bag: Equipment and supplies that porters carry can be packed in sturdy, bright-color (for recognizability) duffel bags, preferably ones that can be secured with a lock.

Numbered locks are easiest – no need to carry a key around.

You can pick up a lot of trekking clothing and gear in Thamel, the globetrotter ghetto of Kathmandu. Be sure to check quality, especially of the seams. Some vendors have high calibre gear leftover from expeditions.

Bring Earplugs (more than one pair as they are easily lost). Homes, lodges, and tents can have remarkably thin walls, and buses/vehicles often have blaring stereos.

Water Heater: At high altitudes, Filling a water bottle with hot water and wrapping it in clothing will make a source of heat that can be kept close to the body or even placed in a sleeping bag for added warmth.

Sunglasses to absorb ultraviolet light. If you wear eyeglasses or contact lenses, bring a spare pair and copy of the prescription in the event replacements are needed.

Leave the pocket knife behind. A Leatherman or Swiss Army Knife gadget combination can be useful but unnecessarily heavy unless the multi-functional tools are needed. Often a simple pocket knife will do if at all.

Umbrellas can be used not only against rainfall but to protect against the sunlight on hot days and also for privacy while answering nature's call.

Collapsible ski poles or walking sticks (lauro in Nepali), often made of lightweight bamboo, can help ease the load and impact on the knees and are found in tourist trekking shops in Thamel.

Bring several handkerchiefs or bandannas. A bandanna can be useful as a makeshift face mask in windy, dusty areas and during vehicle travel, and to dry cups, plates, and hands. You can keep a separate bandana for the usual runny nose that accompanies colds and upper-respiratory infections—or learn to blow your nose Nepali style, covering each nostril in turn and blowing out the other.

Petroleum jelly, Chap Stick, and lip balm are good for cold-weather to prevent or treat chafing.

A supply of duct tape can serve as an all-purpose, temporary fix for various situations. Several feet of tape can be wound around a flashlight handle or water bottle to store for future needs.

Bring and use sunscreen. At high altitude the sun's rays can be especially harsh.

Do not trek alone. Attacks are rare, but when they do happen it is generally against lone trekkers. If you are single, check online and at hotel and restaurant bulletin boards for partners or arrange through a trekking agency.

General Tips for Traveling in Nepal

Bring a universal adapter with you. Electricity averages 220 volts/50 cycles in Nepal. As Nepal becomes increasingly electrified, there are more and more places along the popular routes to recharge. It is considered environmentally ethical to bring spent cells back to your home country for proper disposal.

Have a headlamp and flashlight, especially useful when a regularly scheduled blackout occurs in Kathmandu.

If you play a portable musical instrument, consider bringing it along. A harmonica, recorder, or flute can quickly ease communication barriers. Consider other social and entertainment skills that you can share, for example, portrait drawing and simple magic tricks.

It's a good idea to have a particle mask, to protect against dust and fumes in cities and on bus journeys. They can be found in Kathmandu pharmacies.

Most travelers carry reading and writing materials, and hotels along the popular routes often have paperbacks to sell or trade. A pack of cards and miniature versions of popular board games (such as Scrabble) can be a good way to pass time and liven up a restaurant as well as get to know fellow travelers.

*Please visit **Nepal Trip Advisor, www.nepaltripadvisor.com** for more insider information, and my blog at www.alolyo.wordpress.com.*

ABOUT THE AUTHOR

Alonzo Lyons is author of *Nepal Introduction, The Guerrilla Trek and Yarsa Trails, Nepali for Tourists* and *A Tiny Little Insider's Guide to Pokhara* as well as two forthcoming guidebooks: **The Tongba Trail (aka, Three Cups of Roxy) - A Journey in Remote Eastern Nepal**, and **The Star Trek - A Journey in Rugged Western Nepal**.

He was born and raised in the developing world of Planet Earth (specifically Idaho, NW-USA) and is currently on a quest to admire and report on the secrets and treasures of the Himalaya. Please visit his websites www.alolyo.wordpress.com, www.guerrillatrek.org, and Secrets of the Himalaya (www.sohimalaya.com) for more information or just to say hello.

Good-speed and Keep on Trekking!

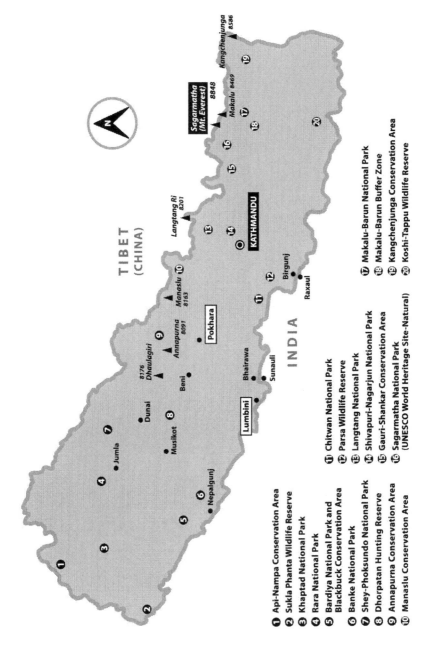

N

TIBET
(CHINA)

Kangchenjunga 8586

Sagarmatha
(Mt. Everest)
8848

Makalu 8469

⑲

⑰

⑱

⑳

⑯

⑮

Langtang Ri
8201

KATHMANDU

◎

⑬

⑭

Birgunj

Raxaul

⑫

⑪

Manaslu 8163

⑩

Pokhara

Annapurna
8091

⑨

8176
Dhaulagiri

INDIA

Beni

Bhairawa

Sunauli

Dunai

Musikot ⑧

Lumbini

Jumla

⑦

④

Nepalgunj

⑥

⑤

③

①

②

❶ Api-Nampa Conservation Area
❷ Sukla Phanta Wildlife Reserve
❸ Khaptad National Park
❹ Rara National Park
❺ Bardiya National Park and
   Blackbuck Conservation Area
❻ Banke National Park
❼ Shey-Phoksundo National Park
❽ Dhorpatan Hunting Reserve
❾ Annapurna Conservation Area
❿ Manaslu Conservation Area

⓫ Chitwan National Park
⓬ Parsa Wildlife Reserve
⓭ Langtang National Park
⓮ Shivapuri-Nagarjun National Park
⓯ Gauri-Shankar Conservation Area
⓰ Sagarmatha National Park
   (UNESCO World Heritage Site-Natural)
⓱ Makalu-Barun National Park
⓲ Makalu-Barun Buffer Zone
⓳ Kangchenjunga Conservation Area
⓴ Koshi-Tappu Wildlife Reserve

131

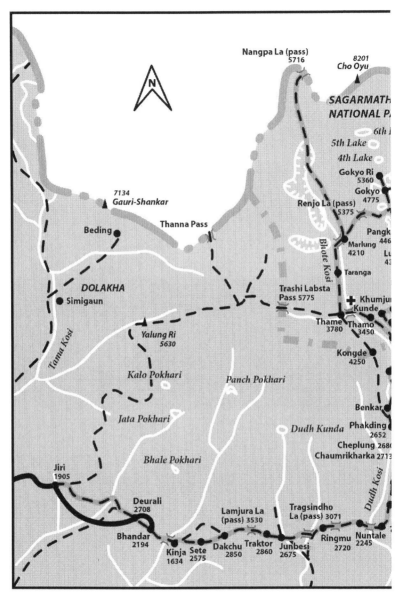

Main Trail

Road

Trail

National Park Boundary

Village/point of interest

Lake/Pond

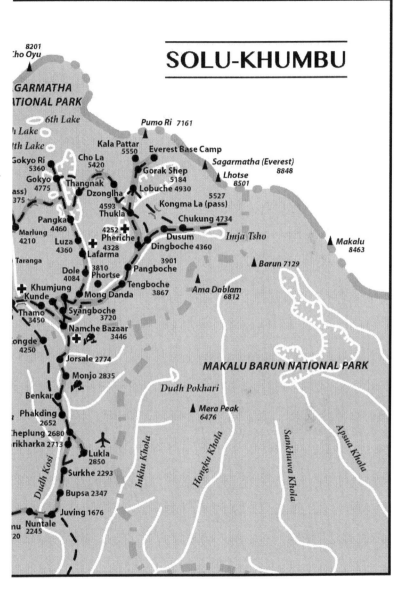

SOLU-KHUMBU

8201
ho Oyu
▲

GARMATHA
TIONAL PARK

6th Lake
h Lake
tth Lake
Gokyo Ri
5360
Gokyo
ass) 4775
375

Cho La
5420

Thangnak

Dzonglha
4593
Thukla

Pumo Ri 7161

Kala Pattar
5550

Gorak Shep
5184

Lobuche 4930

Everest Base Camp

Sagarmatha (Everest)
8848

Lhotse
8501

5527
Kongma La (pass)

Pangka
Marlung 4460
4210
Luza
4360
Taranga

4252
Pheriche
4328
Lafarma

Chukung 4734

Dusum
Dingboche 4360

Imja Tsho

Makalu
8463

Dole
4084
Khumjung
Kunde
Thamo
3450
ongde
4250

3810
Phortse

Mong Danda

Syangboche
3720

Pangboche
3901

Tengboche
3867

Ama Dablam
6812

Barun 7129

Namche Bazaar
3446

Jorsale 2774

Monjo 2835

Benkar
Phakding
2652
heplung 2680
rikharka 2713

Lukla
2850
Surkhe 2293

Bupsa 2347

Juving 1676
nu Nuntale
20 2245

Dudh Pokhari

Mera Peak
6476

Dudh Kosi

Inkhu Khola

Hongku Khola

Sankhuwa Khola

Apsua Khola

MAKALU BARUN NATIONAL PARK

Glacier/Moraine
River/Stream
▲ Mountain/Peak

Check Post
✚ Health Post
✈ Airport

133

Made in the
USA
Columbia, SC